Seamless

Understanding the
Bible as One Complete Story

angie smith

LifeWay Press® Nashville, Tennessee

Published by LifeWay Press® • © 2015 Angie Smith
Reprinted January 2018

ISBN 9781430032304 • Item 005644879

Dewey decimal classification: 220.07
Subject headings: BIBLE—STUDY AND TEACHING \ BIBLE—HISTORY OF BIBLICAL EVENTS

Unless indicated otherwise, all Scripture quotations are taken from The Holy Bible, English Standard Version, copyright © 2000, 2001 by Crossway Bibles, a division of Good News Publishers. Scripture quotations marked HCSB® are taken from the Holman Christian Standard Bible®, Copyright ©1999, 2000, 2002, 2003, 2009 by Holman Bible Publishers. Used by permission. Holman Christian Standard Bible® and HCSB® are federally registered trademarks of Holman Bible Publishers.

To order additional copies of this resource, write to LifeWay Church Resources Customer Service; One LifeWay Plaza; Nashville, TN 37234-0113; order online at *www.lifeway.com;* fax 615.251.5933; phone toll free 800.458.2772; email *orderentry@ lifeway.com;* or visit the LifeWay Christian Store serving you.

Printed in the United States of America

Adult Ministry Publishing • LifeWay Church Resources
One LifeWay Plaza • Nashville, TN 37234-0152

MEET THE AUTHOR

Angie Smith is the wife of Todd (of the Christian music group Selah), and mom to five girls: twins Ellie and Abby, Kate, Audrey, and Charlotte. Many women met Angie through her blog a few years ago when she walked through the difficult days of her daughter Audrey's diagnosis during pregnancy and her brief life. Angie's passion is to make the Bible feel accessible and relevant, to share her ups and downs to encourage others in their faith, and hopefully, to provide a few laughs along the way. She is a best-selling author of two children's books and several adult books, including *I Will Carry You* and *What Women Fear,* and holds a Master's degree in Developmental Psychology from Vanderbilt University. Angie and Todd live with their house full of girls in Nashville.

CONTENTS

INTRODUCTION

SOMETIMES THE MOST MEANINGFUL WRITING DOESN'T HAPPEN IN CHRONOLOGICAL ORDER. AS I SIT TAPPING OUT THESE WORDS, I HAVE JUST RECEIVED THE PDF VERSION OF THIS STUDY IN ITS ENTIRETY.

And I won't bother sugarcoating my response—I sobbed.

Because 15 years ago, I would have told you that Jesus was a myth, a legend, a fairy tale for those who needed a distraction from this life. I would have sounded intellectual, too.

I had degrees, published studies, and years of fancying myself as some sort of expert on life—all at the ripe age of 23. I still see that girl in my mind's eye as I hold this work in my hands, and the irony isn't lost on me.

I wouldn't even walk into a LifeWay store because I was so convinced I wasn't "one of them," and now I'm signing off on my first Bible study with them as my publisher.

And here's the best part: He knew it all along.

He watched me search, cling, and grasp at anything that felt like truth, all the while being well aware that one day I would bow before Him. And the fact that His mercy reaches all the way into the heart of a rebellious, stubborn, undeserving (let me guess, you're starting to feel a little anxious about me being your guide), mess of a woman, well, I can't quite explain what that does to my heart.

The weight of these pages is more than you can feel. It's the love song I never thought I would sing to the Creator who gave me a voice. And while it's not perfect, I pray that it honors Him.

I have had more Bibles than I can count since I began my journey with Him. Many of them are weathered, marked, and littered with notes and prayers. It took me years and years of reading to begin to understand the story of Scripture, but when I began to, the world came into sharp focus for the first time.

Maybe you can relate?

You love the stories you know, but you aren't sure how they fit together. Or maybe you understand it from an academic perspective, but you can't quite get your heart to care.

Or possibly, you've simply done what you could to understand enough to get by in small group, and you go home feeling like you're behind the curve.

A million scenarios could have led you to this study, but whatever the case, I'm praying for you right this minute. You. God knows your name, your circumstances, and exactly what He has in mind for the next several weeks. And I have the great pleasure and distinct honor of joining you in that journey.

Thank you for the privilege—truly. I can only pray that you are as blessed by reading it as I have been by writing it. The Word is alive. It's active. It pierces us, bringing us near to Him and to the cross that freed us.

That's actually in the Bible. It's in the Book of Hebrews. We'll get there.

Of course, that particular book of the Bible doesn't exactly happen in chronological order; but as I said, that's often the way it goes.

Today is a new day for you, my friend.

Circle it on the calendar and mark it in your Bible—whatever you want to do to commit yourself to the days ahead. We're in it together, and I'm cheering you on every single step of the way.

WITH LOVE, ANGIE

WEEK 1
THE BEGINNING

The entire Bible is a vast library, written by 40 authors over 1,600 years. You can explore the nooks and crannies for a lifetime. But the amazing thing is those 66 books tell one seamless story about the God who made us, loves us, redeems us, and has a future for us.

As we journey through Scripture together, we'll use pictures to help see the story unfold before us. Each week, you'll find five icons or pictures at the bottom of the page that represent major moments or turning points in the story. Each day we'll highlight the image that represents the part of the story we are unpacking.

For week 1, we'll be covering the first 11 chapters of the Bible using the icons below to highlight the major themes. The globe represents the creation of the world (Genesis 1). The symbol of man and woman represents the creation of Adam and Eve, the first people (Genesis 2). The snake—yes, you're getting this—Satan and the fall of humanity into sin (Genesis 3 and 4). The boat? Noah and the flood (Genesis 6–9). And the tower? Babel, where God humbled humanity (Genesis 11).

If you look at the back of the book you'll find a fold-out page we call the course map. On that one diagram you can see the icons that summarize our whole study. I hope you'll remember the parts of the Bible long after you've forgotten this study.

Did you notice anything strange about the chapters and icons? Yes, I left out some chapters. Actually Genesis 5 and 10 are pretty much genealogy anyway, but the icons are to help us absorb the main story of the Bible. Also note the days and icons don't always match, but they do tell and picture the story of Scripture in order.

That's enough about the flow and format of the study. Let's get started digging into the beautiful story of Scripture. I'm so glad you've chosen to join me on this journey.

CREATION   MAN & WOMAN   FALL   FLOOD   TOWER

GROUP SESSION GUIDE

Rather than a formal leader guide in the back, we've provided what we hope is a simple and functional group plan on these pages. Each week will begin with an introductory page like the previous one. Then you'll find a two-page group guide like this. My suggestion is that you divide your group time into three parts.

1. After this first week, you'll first discuss the previous week's homework.
2. Then watch the 12-15 minute video segment so I can come along. After all, you wouldn't want to leave me out, would you? Where's the fun in that?
3. Finally, end your group time with a closing discussion of the video. (And of course I'd recommend a party, but that's just me.)

The session guide for this first meeting is for us to get to know each other. Then we'll each go do our homework (it will be fun, I promise). Each day, plan to spend a few minutes with that day's study. Don't worry if some days you don't get it all. This isn't a race and you can come back later. When we meet next group session, we'll have this week's study to discuss. Now let's get to know each other and I'll join you by way of video.

SESSION 1: INTRODUCTION

Getting to know each other:

* What is one thing you want your group to know about you?

Jesus has changed me + everything in my life. Sometimes I'm overwhelmed + need love + understanding

* What drew you to this study?

I need to read the Bible

WATCH SESSION 1: INTRODUCTION (VIDEO RUN TIME 14:54)

DISCUSS:

* How did Angie's experience of feeling lost or stupid trying to study the Bible resonate with you? What have been your own challenges in studying the Bible?

I'm not able to really apply the bible to my life - never really understood

* What do you hope to gain as you study and participate with this group in the coming weeks?

Observe, Interprete + Apply the word to my life and see Gods transformation.

* How as a group can you help one another avoid discouragement and feeling overwhelmed, and stay accountable to stick it out for the whole study?

Understanding + Gentleness.

* What are some steps you will take this week to devote yourself to the work of this study?

Begin to Just Read the bible. I need to Just start!

DAY 1
GETTING STARTED

One of the first things I learned about successfully fitting in with Christians was the power of nodding. It made people think I understood things I didn't, and it covered over the insecurity and frustration of feeling like the Bible was never going to make sense to me. So, when they said things like, "I'm so inspired by Paul's courage," I would bob my head and make a mental note to investigate later.

When they upped the ante with phrases like, "This story takes place in modern-day Iraq," I nodded. I couldn't point at modern-day Iraq on a map if my life depended on it, let alone do the mental bridge-building to get to the part where this realization was as euphoric as it seemed to be for other people.

Have you ever been there? It's all over your head and you're counting the minutes until you can leave the situation that reminds you that you aren't smart enough to "get it."

And it's the worst. *It's the absolute* WORST.

I'm a relatively bright person, and I tend to pick things up (fairly) quickly, but the Bible? That was different. I just couldn't make sense of it.

So many pages. Such thin, thin pages.

Like tissue that taunted me. That's what the Bible was to me for many years: taunting tissue.

I eventually just got so frustrated that I pulled the lens back and walked into my local Christian bookstore. I asked them to point me in the direction of the children's section and I sat cross-legged on the floor thumbing through the bright photos and short summary stories for a few hours.

And don't laugh, because it actually helped me. I bought a few children's storybook Bibles and after I was finished with my classes each day I would sit on the balcony of our apartment and read. Slowly, and without letting the voice of condemnation speak louder than the voice of devotion.

Whatever it takes, Lord. I want to know You and see You in these words.

* *Help a girl out here. Tell me I'm not the only one. What kind of Bible discussions make you feel lost or left out?*

I memorized a few passages and did several amazing Bible studies, but the overarching story escaped me. Details just floated there in space without anything to anchor them down to the bigger picture. It wasn't until I spent time investing in understanding the basic story that the characters and themes of Scripture really came to life for me, and my greatest desire is for this study to do the same for you.

Don't misunderstand me—I am by no means a Bible scholar, and I'm sure I've barely scratched the surface when it comes to understanding the Word, but I've made progress. I know enough about the general story of the Bible to be able to make an educated guess about the where and why of a particular story, and that's an amazing feeling. For example, if you would have asked me where the story of Samuel was, I would have looked in the only place I knew would help me: the index. And I still do that plenty of times, but more often than not, I have enough surrounding information to know the general circumstances of his life to find him.

Now, it looks more like this:

Samuel was the son of Hannah and was raised by Eli the priest. Eli was also a judge, and Samuel would grow up to become the very last judge before the people demanded a king and Saul was placed in that role.

Now I know the general story and time period for this particular person, and understanding who judges and kings were helps me know why his story is significant.

A lot of the time, you know a verse or a story, but you don't know where it lands in the bigger picture, so you miss the significance. Also, if you are confused about what I just said regarding Samuel, don't worry. You're in the right place. And trust me—in a few weeks, you'll be shocked at how you can look at the same sentences and make sense of them.

I'm so excited to travel these roads with you, and prayerfully, you'll make it to the other side with a newfound sense of the architecture of the Word of God.

JUDGES

↓

SAMUEL

↓

SAUL
(FIRST KING)

THE BIBLE
WASN'T
WRITTEN
FOR EXPERTS.

Before we start, though, I want you to make a commitment to really see this through over the next several weeks. Tell yourself right now that you are going to work hard, praying the Holy Spirit will speak to you in new ways as you go. No matter how little (or how much) you know, I pray this study will breathe life into your love for the Word of God, and that it will empower you to claim its promises as your own.

As we go, I want you to remember something very important: the Bible wasn't written for a few experts to understand while baffling the rest of us.

Did you hear that?

The Bible was written for us, and we are claiming that right now, even before we turn a page. With that being the case, I want you to erase any part of your self-talk that says you aren't smart enough or educated enough or even spiritual enough. Deal?

I can't tell you how many people I meet who hang their heads in conversation because they don't think they measure up to other, "smarter" Christians. LISTEN. That's the Devil calling, and we aren't answering. He is no longer going to have that power over our lives. You are capable, intelligent, and loved by the Author of the story. And we're putting our full weight into believing it.

Alright, so we've gotten that out of the way, but a voice in your head may still be whispering another lie about Scripture: it's boring.

In all honesty, there was a time when I would have said the same. But once I made a commitment to read it and to study it, the words became life to me. The reason I thought it was boring was pretty simple: I didn't understand it.

* *How much do you agree with the following statements?*

"I understand the general story of Scripture from Genesis to Revelation."

1   2   3   4   5   6   7   8   9   10

"I feel nervous in settings where my biblical knowledge could be tested."

1   2   3   4   5   6   7   8   9   10

"I've never thought of myself as a student of the Word."

1   2   3   4   5   6   7   8   9   10

"I have a hard time believing I can really understand Scripture the way educated people do."

1   2   3   4   5   6   7   8   9   10

"I've just never really been interested in understanding the Bible as a story."

1   2   3   4   5   6   7   8   9   10

"I wish I felt more confident in my Bible knowledge."

1   2   3   4   5   6   7   8   9   10

"It's just too much for me—too many facts and details to make sense of."

1   2   3   4   5   6   7   8   9   10

"I don't have enough time to read it and try to understand it."

1   2   3   4   5   6   7   8   9   10

* *On the lines below, write anything else you can think of that has kept you from studying the Bible. Maybe you have a lack of confidence, a lack of desire, or any number of other reasons. Let's get them on paper so we know where we're starting and so we can be honest about what we're bringing into this.*

_____

_____

_____

_____

_____

Once you've listed the stumbling blocks and hesitations you have about studying the Bible, take a deep breath and say these words with me:

It's going to be different this time.

We're throwing off anything that has held us back, and we're moving forward in full confidence that He will bless us with the desire of our hearts—to know Him better.

With that, we begin. *Lord, reveal Yourself in every step of this journey, imparting Your wisdom and grace as we go.*

Are you ready? We're going to start at the only logical place to start, which is the beginning.

And just think; in a few weeks, you'll be nodding because you understand, and not because you want to understand. It's going to be a blast to do this together, and I'm so grateful to be next to you.

So there you go—you've already finished day 1. Or, as I would call it if I was actually doing this Bible study instead of writing it, "the first of five sessions I will cram into the hour before I meet with my group."

It's OK, friends.

I'm one of you.

HELPFUL SIGNPOSTS ALONG THE WAY

We're at the beginning of an extraordinary journey, but before we take our first steps, I want to remind you how we'll stay oriented as we go. It's easy to get lost in the details and lose sight of the main points when you're covering so much ground, and I don't want you to leave this study feeling like it was a big jumble of information that you can't simplify. I mean, we've got to know where we're going, where we are, and where we've been, right? (And all my fellow "I consider myself adventurous if by 'adventurous' we mean 'aware of the exact plan'" sisters nod in glee.)

As we all know, visuals can only help the process. So our amazing designer created these fantastic little icons that you'll see at the bottom of the pages to help us stay on track. And when I saw them, I squealed and shouted, "They're ADORABLE!!!!! I LOVE THE PINK!" I have no solid evidence to back up my theory, but I believe that was the biblical response.

Each week we will have 5 icons to indicate the "main points," and in the back of your book, you'll find a course map on the inside back cover (it folds out!) so you can see the entire Bible in pictorial form. Go ahead. SQUEAL WITH ME.

DAY 2
CREATION & FALL

"In the beginning…"
GENESIS 1:1

Three simple words launch us into the pages of God's love for us. The first book of the Bible is called "Genesis," and you would be hard-pressed to find a fiction book with as many twists and turns as Genesis holds. In the first several verses we learn the order in which God created all things.

There's a handy little doodad on the sidebar to see what God created on each of the 7 days, but we're going to hone in on the beginning of humanity.

God created Adam (the first man) from the dust of the earth. I don't know a whole lot more about how that went down, but the bottom line is God created this man in God's own image. He wanted this person to reflect Him and to be a beautiful representation of the way He loves.

God wanted Adam to have a partner, so He put Adam into a deep sleep, removed one of his ribs and used it to create Eve—the woman who would be Adam's wife.

I have a friend who has a tattoo on his rib cage devoted to his wife. It's a sticky note that reads, "You owe me one."

I think it's clever.

Anyway, Adam's new wife brings some issues into the marriage. Namely, the fact that she doesn't act like she's 100% sure she trusts God. Don't think this is a women-bashing session. I assure you it isn't. But facts are facts, and the first lady of the garden did her fair share of disobeying.

We label that original disobedience against God with a big theological term: the fall. Four letters, but trust me, it's a big term.

* *From what you know, what resulted from the original act of disobedience against God—the fall?*

1 LIGHT/DARK & DAY/NIGHT

2 SKY/HEAVEN

3 EARTH/SEAS & PLANTS

4 SUN/MOON/ STARS

5 BIRDS/FISH

6 LAND ANIMALS & HUMANS

7 REST

    CREATION

Everything was going swimmingly for Adam and Eve. They had a great place to live and all of their needs were met. But even from the beginning of time, there was the question that haunts us to this day: "Does God really have my best in mind?"

☐ GENESIS=
   the beginning

God had been clear in His instructions: anything was fair game to eat with the exception of the fruit from one particular tree. Well, we humans buck anything that feels like a limitation on our "rights."

So Satan, clothed as a snake, shimmies into the picture and plants a seed of doubt in Eve's mind.

✱ *What does Satan ask Eve in Genesis 3:1?*

✱ *How would you describe Satan's approach in verses 2-7?*

Do you see how subtle he is? How conniving? How he undermines God and presents what feels like a logical case?

Yeah. He still does that.

Eve falls for it. She decides the fruit is a good thing—after all, why wouldn't a loving God want her to have this fantastic knowledge? So she takes a bite and hands one to Adam. And everything changes. Forever.

I'm not just trying to be dramatic—it really was the turning point for humanity.

God created a situation where His people could choose whether or not to live in accordance with His rules. They chose not to. That decision shaped every person who would ever be born after them, because their disobedience resulted in separation from God. God is perfect, so the stain of sin put them (and us) in a state of opposition from Him. In and of ourselves, we do not have the power to bridge that gap.

Now listen, I know we're starting out with some pretty heady stuff here, and if it were up to me I might have eased us into it. I wonder if you're already sorting through questions in your mind, "Were they literally seven 24-hour days?," "Were Adam and Eve real people?," and probably many others. So let's take this opportunity to deal with another big issue we're going to face as we go so the elephant in the room doesn't impede our main goal.

If we are genuinely seeking the glory of God, let's agree for the time being to set down all of our preconceived notions and the bits and

 MAN & WOMAN

pieces of arguments that have influenced our opinions. That's certainly not to say you shouldn't have those opinions, or that it's even an option to be wishy-washy, but I bring this up so that you don't miss the heart of what we're doing here. I'm not taking the easy way out, and I will volunteer my own thoughts, but I have seen the way pride and power can corrupt the purity of the Word of God. Many times, I have spoken out of a place that was more concerned with being right before men than it was of being right before God.

And many times, I just wanted to know the answer so I would feel like I had figured it out. That's my safety zone right there—control. But above and beyond any of my lofty desires is this unshakable reality: I do not and will never know everything there is to know, nor was I created to understand all the mysteries of God.

It's not a cop-out to say you're clothing yourself in humility and seeking His voice. So before you get any further, spend just a moment praying over anything that rises up in you in an attempt to discredit the Word. Make a commitment to yourself and to God that this study is not a place for wrestling out every question you have, but rather an opportunity to grow in knowledge. There will be plenty of opportunities for you to take what you learn and apply it, but the heart of this study is to come to the Lord with our hearts open, refusing to let a defensive stance prevent us from growth.

* *Write down any thoughts that come to mind, asking the Lord to bless you as you seek Him in these next weeks.*

You may not feel like we covered a lot of ground in this first section, but we've introduced the thread that will weave its way through the end of time.

Sin took root in the garden of Eden, and it will grow into a monstrosity before God, in His mercy, will send His Son to us.

FALL

DAY 3
RESULTS OF THE FALL

After their disobedience, Adam and Eve were filled with shame, suddenly aware of their nakedness and fearful of the consequences of sin. They attempted to hide themselves from God and as they did, God asked His own "first question."

✳ *What did God ask in Genesis 3:9?*

Now listen. He's God. He knows all things, so He isn't actually trying to figure out where they've gone.

✳ *What do you think God was actually getting at here?*

You could probably supply a couple of good answers to this question, but in my mind the gist of it is that God wasn't asking them to identify their location, but rather their condition. In effect He was asking: "Where are your hearts? What in the world are you thinking, imagining that you can so blatantly disregard Me and then hide?"

As you read through Scripture, I want you to challenge yourself to start thinking critically about the passages and applying them to yourself instead of seeing each story as a far-removed history lesson.

✳ *In other words, when you read the question, "Where are you?" imagine that He's talking to you. Take a moment and jot in the margin the first responses that come to your mind. Don't edit yourself or worry about sharing this publicly—this is just between you and Him. Are you hiding? Ashamed? Doubting? Be honest.*

No matter what you wrote, know this: it is not a surprise to God. He knows where you are exactly as He knew where they were—body, soul,

FALL

mind, and spirit. What He wants from you is the same as what He wanted from them: to come to Him, no matter how difficult it seems, instead of allowing Satan to continue oppressing you with lies.

I wish I could say I didn't see myself in what happens next, but of course I do. God spoke again to Adam and Eve, asking them to give an account. Adam started out on the right path.

* *What does Adam say in Genesis 3:10?*

In other words? I screwed up, and then I really regretted it.

Good place to start when you're chatting with the God of the universe who breathed life right into your lungs.

But when God starts to corner Adam and he can feel the weight of that sin on his chest, he does something *I would never do* (untrue).

* *Whom does Adam blame? (Genesis 3:12)*

❏ *the dog*   ❏ *Eve*   ❏ *God*
❏ *both Eve and God*   ❏ *Eve, God, and the dog*

Oh, clever, Adam. Way to throw in the, "You're the One who gave her to me" part. I'd say Adam blamed both his wife and God. Adam has his finger pointing at Eve, who evidently also minored in "passing the buck" at the University of Eden.

* *Whom does she blame? (Genesis 3:13)*

He tricked me! I call foul! I mean, how was I supposed to know all of this would happen? The trouble was and is that neither Eve nor we are helpless victims. We always have the choice to believe either God or the Devil. It can't be both.

Next, God speaks to the serpent, and within this text we find the first reference to Jesus, the Savior who will be sent to restore our relationship with God. In Genesis 3:15, we read:

FALL

I will put enmity between you and the woman,
and between your offspring and her offspring;
he shall bruise your head,
and you shall bruise his heel.
GENESIS 3:15

Adam and Eve could not understand these words from the vantage point that we (in possession of the whole of Scripture) now have, but the heart of what God is saying is this:

Satan will bruise the heel of God's people—he will wound them and have a negative effect on their lives. He is the enemy of God and the Devil will always do his best to injure and mislead God's children. But a wound to the heel is not lethal; it is temporary.

On the other hand, crushing the head of a serpent results in death. It's interesting to note that a snake's poison is in its head, so the power to inflict injury is erased when the head is destroyed.

Here we see a promise from God, spoken just after His creation has gone astray: *The state you have placed yourself in is temporary, and out of my deep love for you, despite how little you deserve it, I will bring a solution to bridge the chasm between us.*

* *Do you think this promise from God eliminates the earthly repercussions we suffer if we're disobedient to Him? Why or why not?*

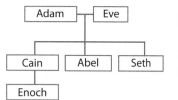

Does this eliminate repercussions? I would say no. Indeed God speaks directly to both Adam and Eve, detailing the ways that their sin will continue to affect all generations to come. Read Genesis 3:16-19 to see the specific ways they (and we) will be affected.

After God sends Adam and Eve out of the garden, we see the pattern of sin continue in their children. The world's first murder takes place as one of their sons (Cain) kills the other (Abel) out of anger. Cain marries and has a son of his own (Enoch), and some time later Adam and Eve give birth to another son (Seth).

Does anything in that last paragraph strike you as odd? Did you wonder where Cain got his wife? After all, we've been given the names of two sons of Adam and Eve, and given that they are the only humans on the planet at this point, where did Cain's wife come from?

 FALL

The answer appears in Genesis 5:4, where we read "The days of Adam after he fathered Seth were 800 years; and he had other sons and daughters." In other words, not all of their children are named, and it is to be assumed that Cain was married to (and produced children with) one of his sisters.

It's not like there were a lot of choices on his eHarmony® app, that's all I'm saying.

Please note: we are about to dig into some lineage. We're looking at who was born to whom and why that will eventually matter. If you feel the need to grab another cup of coffee and give yourself a quick pep talk, I'll be waiting right here for you.

One of the descendants from Seth was named Enoch. Yes, the same name as Cain's son, apparently they hadn't mastered the art of naming children at that point. Enoch was recognized as being a man who loved the Lord.

✳ *What three words in Genesis 5:22-24 describe Enoch's relationship with God?*

If you're anything like me, your tendency is to glance over the long list of names and continue to skim until something that seems important and relevant shows up.

✳ *But the truth is, having an idea of how much time passed between people and events is really helpful to seeing the big picture, so just take a few minutes and fill in the following names from Genesis 5:21-32.*

Enoch fathered _____,
who fathered _____,
who fathered _____,
who fathered, _____, _____,
and _____.

See? It's not so bad.

Unfortunately, the conditions of humanity continued to decline, until we come to the words in Genesis 6:5-8.

FALL

The LORD saw that the wickedness of man was great in the earth, and that every intention of the thoughts of his heart was only evil continually. And the LORD regretted that he had made man on the earth, and it grieved him to his heart. So the LORD said, "I will blot out man whom I have created from the face of the land, man and animals and creeping things and birds of the heavens, for I am sorry that I have made them." But Noah found favor in the eyes of the LORD.

GENESIS 6:5-8

God is taking stock of the way His creation is behaving, and He is grieved by how far from Him they have wandered. Knowing the depths of their hearts, He recognizes that this will continue to worsen, alienating them further and further from Himself. As a result, He determines the best way to deal with it is to wipe out creation.

I'm sure this comes across as an aggressive strategy, and actually, it is meant to. There is nothing passive about our Father God, and inasmuch as He is good, He is also just. You might be tempted to cross your arms at this point, shaking your head at a God who would destroy His own creation. While I agree that it's a drastic approach, I would urge you to keep in mind one teeny-tiny-itsy-bitsy detail.

We aren't God.

That means we can't "put ourselves in His place," and any attempts to apply our own standards and expectations on Him are basically futile. He is entirely separate from us, and fully sovereign—meaning He can do what He wants when He wants. He is also fully love so what He does is ultimately loving whether we can presently understand or not.

But (and this is important), He cannot go against His nature or His promises, and as we will see in the coming weeks, He has given us more than enough information on those to give us a secure faith.

I realize we've made it a grand total of 6 chapters so far, and you're probably wondering how in the world we're going to move to a good understanding of Scripture in one study if we keep up this pace. Don't worry—we'll get there. But the foundation we are laying will help you to think critically as you read, and the time we have spent here will serve us well as we build up our knowledge base.

FLOOD

* *As you close out this section, spend some time in prayer, focusing on any concerns or struggles you have with the text so far. Are you unsettled by anything? Curious? Confused? Speak honestly and thoroughly with the Lord. Ask Him to give you eyes to see Him in all His splendor as we continue to journey through Scripture.*

Also, that was a long lesson. My apologies.

It's just that I'm trying to cram the whole Bible into six sessions and I'm realizing it may have been a bit, *ahem,* ambitious.

Stick with me. We'll get there.

SO FAR:
GOD CREATED
THE WORLD

↓

GOD
CREATED
PEOPLE

↓

ADAM + EVE
SINNED

↓

THE FALL PUT
ALL CREATION
UNDER
THE CURSE
OF SIN

FLOOD

DAY 4
THE FLOOD

So where were we? Oh yes. God was about to destroy the earth and kill everyone. How's your day so far?

Actually, He wasn't going to kill everyone, but very few people were chosen to survive. Namely, Noah and his family.

God speaks to Noah, telling him that He is going to send a great flood, and that Noah is to build an ark to take his family to safety. Along with his wife, sons, and daughters-in-law, Noah is also instructed to bring seven pairs of every kind of clean animal and one pair of every kind of unclean animal as well as seven pairs of every kind of bird in order to keep them alive and reproducing for generations to come.

God gives Noah detailed information on the exact dimensions of the ark as well as the materials to be used and the other preparations that should be taken before the flood comes.

* How long did it rain? (Genesis 7:4)

Here's a Bible trivia tidbit for you. Every time the number 40 is used in Scripture, it indicates a time of testing.

* The water didn't dry up after 40 days, it just stopped raining then. How long did it take for the water to dissipate? (Genesis 7:24)

And do you know what *that* number signifies in Scripture? Sorry. Build-up for no good reason. I actually don't know that it symbolizes anything other than the fact that they were on the boat much of a year (see Genesis 8:14), and I'm just saying that's a lot of quality family time.

Once they do get off the boat, what's the first thing they do? (Find a therapist! No, that's not it.) Read Genesis 8:20.

* Noah built an _____ and offered _____ _____.

 FLOOD

This brings us to one of the central themes of Scripture: the use of sacrifice as a symbol of our need for atonement.

> Atonement: *the reconciliation between God and humankind ultimately accomplished through Jesus Christ.*

* *Look back a few chapters to Genesis 3:21. What was the first sacrifice made, and who made it? For what purpose?*

SACRIFICE SHOWS OUR NEED TO BE MADE RIGHT WITH GOD

We're going to talk more about animal sacrifices and their symbolism later (Giddyup!), but for now just be aware of the following:
1. Animal sacrifices were modeled by God and required by Him.
2. Because of this, Noah's immediate action after returning to land was seen as honorable and good, and was recognized as such by God, who called it a "pleasing aroma." (Genesis 8:21)

You know what probably wasn't a "pleasing aroma"? The inside of the boat. I've cried uncle after a six-hour road trip with my kids for goodness' sake.

* *God blesses Noah for his faithfulness, and then He tells him to do something. What is it? (Genesis 9:1)*

Be _____ and _____ and

_____ _____ _____.

Go on. Have kids. Have lots of kids. Let's try this whole humanity in God's image thing over again.

And God is also making His end of the bargain clear: I'm never going to do this again. I will never flood the earth this way again. Ever.

* *What does He use as a symbol of His promise? (Genesis 9:13)*

 FLOOD

Now, maybe you just saw an image in your mind of a pretty little rainbow, and it's taking the edge off the whole mass destruction part, but you're not all that inclined to be moved by the gesture. But what it signifies is something profound and entirely indicative of the enduring love that God has for His people, and a reminder to us that He has chosen to be in relationship with us.

Still not excited about the rainbow? Let me say it in another way, and I'm praying you hear it as the heartbeat of this study. Even when we didn't deserve it, God gave us another chance. In the roar of your own sense of entitlement, you might miss what that actually means.

God doesn't owe us a single thing.

It's His show, y'all. Every bit of it.

And as much as you might intrinsically recoil at that statement, I promise you this: the greatest freedom and joy you will ever know are wrapped up in God's work, offered as a gift from the King of all kings.

Nothing else from here on out will land where it's supposed to if you don't at least have the desire to understand that truth. It's the reason we argue about secondary issues as the body of Christ—we've fundamentally missed the whole point of the story.

God doesn't have to love you, but He does.

You can't do anything to earn it, because you're flawed in ways that make your best efforts completely useless.

In the quietness of your own heart, I want you to consider this mental perspective shift. Instead of wondering why He did something as drastic as killing an entire world of people, ask yourself a more pressing question: *why did He let anyone live?*

So often, we go into situations in life with our fists up, ready to defend our rights and our opinions, but this is one area where attempting to do so is dangerous. I'm sorry to be such a party pooper, and I promise things are going to get better as we go. It's not going to be a pound-you-over-the-head kind of study, but if we don't lay it out here, we might not fully appreciate the beauty that lies up ahead.

And believe me, it is beautiful.

 FLOOD

DAY 5
JOB & BABEL

I'm going to take what appears to be a rabbit trail here, but it's actually not. One of the reasons the Bible is hard to understand as one complete story is that it didn't necessarily happen in the order we read it.

For example, the Book of Job was written about a man named Job who suffered immensely, losing his family, his health, and his wealth in a very short amount of time. If you look in your table of contents, you'll see that it's the 18th book of the Bible, nowhere near where we are in the Book of Genesis.

But actually, Job's story probably happened right around where we are in this chapter. Historians have indicated that based on the language and other cues given, Job lived sometime shortly after the flood.

I think Job is one of the most difficult books of the Bible to understand, to embrace, and to teach.

* *Read Job 1:6-12 and write a brief summary of what is happening.*

EVENTS SO FAR:
* God created:
  * the world
  * Adam and Eve
* Sin wrecked everything
* The world went downhill until God sent the flood
* God started over with Noah
* Job believed God is good even through suffering

God gives permission to Satan to do whatever he wants to with Job, so long as he doesn't kill him. With bated breath, we watch as Satan strips Job's life away from him, and if we are honest, we are tempted to be angry about it.

Why would God allow such a thing? What kind of loving God would willingly let one of His loved ones to be treated this way?

I know. I hear you. I've asked the same. It feels cruel and unnecessary as we turn the pages, but all I know to say is this: I believe God is good even when I don't understand all the particulars of His decisions.

I don't say this flippantly. I say it as a woman who has stood in a cemetery while her daughter was being buried.

And with the thud of every shovelful of dirt that separated us, I had a decision to make about the God who allowed it: either He loves me or He doesn't. Either He is good or He is not.

☐ JOB =
faithfulness amidst suffering

TOWER

I decided to believe God is good, and He loves me. It wasn't a decision based on emotion or shallow hope—it was, quite simply, the only place I found safe enough to rest my weary bones.

I'm willing to bet you've had some Job-like moments in your life, and maybe they've been what led to you losing faith. Your Heavenly Father isn't afraid of your questions, your doubt, or your frustration, and maybe this is a good place to just camp out with Him for a few minutes before we finish.

Again, this is for you and the Lord, so be honest.

* *What experiences in your life have caused you to struggle with believing He is good and that He loves you? Write these down on a separate sheet of paper and then seal it up, so you can feel free to write just to God.*

This is just between you and Him. Talk to Him, not to anyone else. Maybe they are things you've never even put pen to paper about, but this is your chance. Talk to Him … He's listening.

Good for you, friend. I know that wasn't easy. We're tucking this away for now, but not forever.

Take a deep breath. Let's wrap up this lesson together, OK?

* *Noah's three sons, named _____, _____, and _____ (Genesis 9:18) had children, those children had children, and eventually the world began to fill up with people again.*

* *Read Chapter 11 of Genesis for yourself and then fill in the following: (Answers will vary slightly depending on the Bible translation you are using, but that's OK. You'll get the heart of the message!)*

The whole earth had _____ _____. (v. 1)

They said, let us build _____ and make a _____ for ourselves. (v. 4)

 TOWER

It didn't take too long for people to move in ways that elevated themselves and not God, did it? When God saw this happening, He intervened again by dispersing the people and confusing their language.

You may have heard this story before, as its name is famous, but now you'll have some context for the "Tower of Babel." It was a monument that stood for man's desire to be important, and when God scrambled their ability to understand language and had them spread out instead of building power together, He was reinforcing our need for humility.

Before we end this week's lesson, take a few minutes to consider what you've learned, praying that God will continue to strengthen the foundation that will lead to steady building in the coming weeks.

* *Put the following events in order (try to do this from memory, but skim your notes if you need to!):*

    _____ *The first murder occurs*

    _____ *Sin enters the world*

    _____ *God creates Adam*

    _____ *God floods the world*

    _____ *The Tower of Babel is built*

    _____ *People are scattered and their language is confused*

* *If you had to summarize the main storyline of Genesis up to here, how would you do it? Think about the nature of man and the nature of God as you answer, being aware of patterns that you've already seen thus far.*

Answers to the ordering exercise: 3, 2, 1, 4, 5, 6

TOWER

two

WEEK 2
THE PATRIARCHS

Good for you. You've been on a tour of prehistory, from the creation of the universe through the Tower of Babel. And you can remember them with the pictures. The globe for creation. The male/female symbol for the creation of the first humans. The snake brings to mind the events and effects of the fall. The boat for Noah and the tower for Babel, and you've got a grip on the whole time period.

Ready for a new week? Let's get started.

We're going to look at the time Bible folks call the period of the patriarchs. In the Bible we're talking Genesis 12 through the end of the book (Genesis 50). We'll not only find out what a patriarch is, we'll get to know them personally. And once again we'll have a set of pictures as a memory aid.

This week we'll begin with a megaphone because God called a man named Abram to begin the redemptive process. We'll see a name tag because God changed Abram's name to Abraham and his grandson Jacob's name to Israel. Israel? Hey, doesn't that name ring a bell? Stick with us and we'll see how it all fits.

Next we see a number 12. Hmmm. Twelve sons of that Israel guy. And 12 tribes of Israel. Do we see a pattern here?

A money bag. Is somebody going to make a profit? Well, only in a manner of speaking. The money bag will remind us of a bunch of brothers who sold their sibling. Haven't we all at least thought about that one at one time or another?

The final icon that pictures our study this week is some pyramids. Somebody's going to Egypt I do believe.

THE CALL   RENAMED   12 TRIBES   SOLD   EGYPT

SESSION 2: THE BEGINNING

REVIEW WEEK 1 HOMEWORK

* What new truths did you learn from your homework this week?

* Day 1: In the past, what kinds of things have been obstacles to your studying the Bible?

* Day 2: From what you know, what resulted from the original act of disobedience against God (the fall)?

* Day 3: What do you think God was actually asking when He called to Adam, "Where are you?" in Genesis 3:9? In what ways do you think God calls to us in the same way?

  • Why do you suppose Adam and Eve so quickly tried to blame someone else for their actions? In what ways do you see us doing the same thing?

  • Do you think the promise of redemption eliminates the earthly repercussions we suffer if we're disobedient to Him? Why or why not?

* Day 4: What promise from the story of Noah does the rainbow represent?

  • What aspect of the Noah story impacts you most? Why?
    a. the severity of God's judgment on sin
    b. the lengths to which God went to preserve Noah
    c. Noah's obedience
    d. the sacrifices Noah offered after the flood
    e. something else

* Day 5: What experiences in your life have caused you to struggle with believing God is good and that He loves you?

WATCH SESSION 2: THE BEGINNING (VIDEO RUN TIME 15:33)

DISCUSS

* What comes to mind when you think about God?

* How are you inspired by the story of the mansion and the truth of authenticity?

* What has been your take on the Bible up to this point? How have you believed it to be true or false?

* In what ways did you gain new understanding of who God is? Of His Word, the Bible?

DAY 1
ABRAM & THE COVENANT

You made it through the first week! Congratulations. Now fasten your seatbelt—God has a thrill ride for us this week.

God scattered the nations after the Tower of Babel, so now we have people all over the place. In a town called Ur lives a man named Terah.

* *Of whom was Terah a descendant? (Genesis 11:10)*

We don't know much about Noah's son Shem, but we learn a little bit in one story in Genesis 9:18-27. Evidently, Noah got drunk and ended up naked in his tent (I'm reporting the facts here, people). One of his sons, Ham, saw him naked and then told his brothers what was going on.

* *What did they do in Genesis 9:23?*

Well done, boys. Cover your drunk and naked dad and show him some respect. Shem was one of the good kids who got his dad's blessing after this incident, and several generations later, Terah was born in his family line.

* *Read Genesis 11:31 and record the following:*

* *Where did they start?*

* *Where did they plan to end up?*

* *Where did they actually end up?*

Look at the map on page 38 to get a sense of their journey. Terah dies in Haran, but his son Abram and Abram's wife Sarai are about to get a pivotal assignment from God.

If this were a movie, the soundtrack music would crescendo right here. We're about to meet a guy God will use more than almost anyone else in the history of the world. Violinists? Cellists? It's go time.

 CALLED

HELLO 12 $ ▲▲

THE CALL OF ABRAM

Genesis 12 is one of the most important chapters in the entire Bible. If you miss what's happening in these few paragraphs, you can't fully understand the rest of the Bible. Intense, right? But also, true.

I bet you know his name, and you might even know a clever song or two about his sons (His name will change to Abraham, but at this point, it's still "Abram."), but it's so much more than that. Here, in a short account of God's words to Abram, we see the first stitch in the seamless story of God's love for a chosen group of people.

GOD CALLED ABRAHAM

↓

TO CREATE ISRAEL

↓

TO GIVE BIRTH TO JESUS

↓

TO SAVE YOU

* Go ahead and read Genesis 12:1.

* Who is speaking to Abram?

* Where/whom does He tell Abram to leave?

* Where does He tell Abram he will end up?

Perfect. Leave everything and go somewhere that I'm not exactly going to specify right this second. Dear control freak: it's time to go night-night for a little bit.

But. BUT!

* What does verse 2 tell us will happen?

"I will make of you a great _____, and I will _____ you and make your_____ great, so that you will be a _____."

* Well, that's a silver lining. What does Abram do in response? (v. 4) _____ _____.

We're going to see this a lot in the coming weeks, and I want you to start paying attention to these short (but awesome) sentences. Over and over, you're going to see a theme of obedience by God's finest men and women, and a majority of the time it's not because they have all the details. It's because they trust God. I don't know about you, but I could stand a few more "she went" moments in my own life.

CALLED

In verse 5, we see where Abram is headed. Where is it?

Pops died in Haran, but Abram gets to Canaan. Then God tells him a little something that will only shape the rest of the Bible and history.

What does God tell Abram He is going to do? (v. 7)

I mean … are you freaking out? No, I know. Hang on—we'll get there.

In our efforts to become friends with the maps, I want you to do a little project. Read Genesis 12:4-9 again and trace over the route of Abram on the map below. I just want you to feel some ownership about all this, and I think that physically drawing it out will help. Start where Abram does and then trace his path.

In case you're wondering, the area pictured in the map below is modern day Egypt on the south, Iraq on the east, and Israel in the middle.

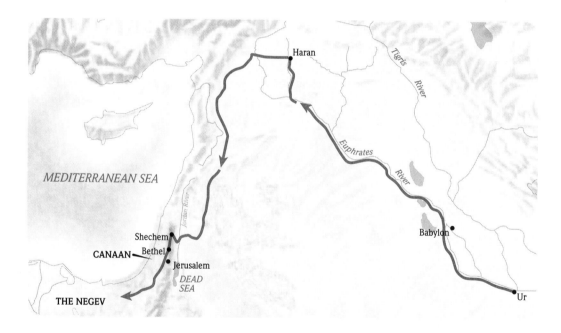

CALLED

When I was in sixth grade, we had to color a map of the United States with colored pencils, including all the major rivers and mountains. I despise geography, but I'd do anything for an excuse to color code things. In fact, I could live at Staples® and be a very happy girl. I daresay Noah wouldn't have bothered getting hammered if he had simply had access to some highlighters and a pack of multi-sized sticky notes.

I digress.

* *Abram and his family don't hang out long. What's going on in verse 10?*

Because of this (again, look at the map so you have a reference point), Abram briefly moves his family to Egypt, but he makes the mistake of lying to the ruler in Egypt (called a Pharaoh), telling him that his wife Sarai is just his sister.

Why, you ask?

Because she was evidently a pretty hot lady and he thought they would kill him to have a shot with her.

Turns out pretending your wife is your sister is a bad idea. The Pharaoh (ruler of Egypt) falls in love with hottie Sarai and gets a tad annoyed when he realizes her "brother" is actually her spouse.

He sends them out of Egypt and they return to Canaan.

I don't know exactly what the soundtrack plays when we've lied about this sort of thing, but whatever that is, it's playing.

For the record, I will say this: Abram wasn't totally lying.

* *What does Genesis 20:12 reveal?*

Don't you feel better now? Phew! I mean, close call on the lying thing. This is much better.

Eww.

Once they get back to Canaan, the land can't sustain both Abram and his nephew, Lot. They decide to split up and Abram tells Lot to choose the land he wants. Abram will take whatever's left.

Lot makes a bad decision and points to the valley region near the Dead Sea because he thinks it will be the most fertile. Unfortunately, it's not only geographically low but also morally low. In a short amount of time God will destroy Sodom because of its wickedness. Do you know the story of Lot? It's not the easiest one to summarize for a kid's Bible, I'll tell you that much.

CALLED

* *Real quickly, jump to Genesis 19:23-26. What does Lot's wife do and what happens as a result?*

The next part isn't any better. His daughters get him drunk and sleep with him. I wanted to sugarcoat that, but facts are facts. The truth is, we will understand stories we read about later if we learn this stuff.

* *So they both get pregnant, and the older daughter names her son _____ and he becomes the father of the _____.(v. 37)*

* *The younger daughter names her son _____ and he becomes the father of the _____. (v. 38)*

Mom is salt and dad is the father of their kids. It might not be the best year ever for the girls. We'll hear of these families again, but just note that this is where they got their start.

GOD'S COVENANT WITH ABRAM

Go back to Genesis 15, where God establishes His covenant with Abram. A covenant is a promise, and that's what this is—but it's so much more. I know this is still unfolding, but Abram will become the father of the chosen people of God. They're special to Him, and most of the Bible will revolve around them, so pay attention.

* *In Genesis 15:5, what does God tell Abram will happen?*

Well, that's fantastic, but also unlikely because Abram has no children.

Not to mention, he's an old *(old)* man. His wife Sarai is well past her childbearing years. This seems like an impossible prediction, yet God is abundantly clear: you will have children. Look at the actual process that God goes through to make this promise to Abram in chapter 15. Go ahead and read that chapter. (Don't cringe. It's not long.)

When two people were in agreement about a covenant, they would take part in a ritual. The Hebrew word for covenant is *barath,* and to enter it, the two parties would divide a sacrifice (translation—they would kill animals, cut them in half, and walk a figure eight pattern together between the bodies while reciting the conditions of the covenant).

CALLED   HELLO   12 $ ▲▲

But this time, something was a little different, because after all, it's God we're talking about, not just two people.

* *In Genesis 15:12, what do we learn about Abram's condition during this process?*

Exactly. Abram was not even awake during the process. That means God made the covenant with Abram—God is obligated to uphold His end of the promise—it was not a mutual arrangement. God takes all the responsibility; only He can keep this promise. Basically, God is saying, "No matter what, My promise stands." Abram didn't need to be a part of it, because God's commitment to Abram was what mattered.

Are you wondering why it's so important that God cut covenant with Abram? Are you thinking, *She is really belaboring this one little story*? If you are, that makes me happy, because it means you are well on your way to realizing that in this moment, God made a promise He will keep for all time, and one that affects our lives today.

This moment, this spectacular moment where God made a commitment to Abram—believe me when I say this: it explains stories you may very well watch on the news tonight. The legacy that began on a mountain between an imperfect man and a perfect God—well, its repercussions spread into the crevices of our lives and faith even as I write these words. Yes. It's that important.

As we close for today, just know this: you've opened the Book of promise, and you're on your way to learning how to understand the rest of it. In this lesson, we met Abram—the man God would use to shape His story forever.

Violinists, take a breath. But not for long, because we're going to need you again in a minute.

CALLED

DAY 2
ISHMAEL AND ISAAC

✳ *If you haven't already, go ahead and read Genesis 15. In verse 13, what does God tell Abram will happen to his offspring? We'll come back to this in a bit, but make a note of it here.*

Abram rushes home to his wife and tells her what he's heard from God. Picture it with me. She's a senior citizen, and her husband comes home with the news that God is going to open her barren womb. Bless her elderly heart, that's a lot to take in with your Metamucil®.

ISHMAEL

Several years pass and Sarai doesn't get pregnant. She decides that the best plan is to take matters into her own hands (because isn't that always the best plan? Umm, no.).

She tells Abram to father a child with her maidservant Hagar. Because Hagar worked for Sarai, the child would be considered hers. As far as she was concerned, this was the only way God's promise could come to fruition—after all, how could a woman in her eighties have a baby?

So, Abram does exactly that, and Hagar conceives. While Hagar is pregnant, she feels mistreated by Sarai and decides to run away. After she's gained some ground, God speaks to her.

✳ *Read Genesis 16:7-15. What does God tell her about the son that will soon be born to her?*

"He shall be a wild donkey of a man." Well that's basically what every mom-to-be wants to hear, isn't it? At least it narrows the ideas for a baby shower theme. After donkey-boy Ishmael is born, Abram hears from God again, and this time He's getting a name change.

✳ *What was Abram's new name? (Genesis 17:1-8)*

 CALLED

God is reminding Abram of His promise. He is reinforcing the fact that, no matter how unlikely it seems, His word will stand. Abram and Sarai will become parents.

It's a happy talk so far.

Abram is now Abraham (meaning "the father of nations") and he's been given some fresh hope. In the next few verses, it gets intense.

Read Genesis 17:9-14. What does verse 11 instruct Abraham to do as a sign of his covenant with God?

Cue the sound of a record scratching. WHAT?

I know. It's not an ideal moment for Abraham. God is telling him that not only does he need to be circumcised at his ripe old age, but so does every male in his family including their slaves.

We can't (unfortunately) skip over this part, because once we get to the New Testament, we'll want to have this knowledge. Maybe I could kick us off with a question?

Why in the world does God tell Abraham to be circumcised along with the rest of his family? (There's no space for you to write in here because it was rhetorical, but feel free to ponder it at your leisure.)

It seems like an odd request—I understand. But here's what you need to know: in Scripture, "the flesh" is used to describe our sinfulness as humans, and this procedure involves cutting away of the flesh. It is therefore a symbol of their need for God and commitment to Him.

Then God tells Abraham that Sarai will now be called "Sarah," and tells him they will have a son together.

What does God tell Abraham about this boy? (v. 19)

Abraham invites all of his male family members to a party they'll never forget. He makes sure that every one of them is circumcised, including his 99-year-old self.

ISAAC

Shortly after this, three angels come to Sarah and Abraham's home, and announce that within a year, Isaac will be born. Sarah, who is out of their eyesight but within the range of their voices, begins to laugh.

A couple of Bible stories make me smile when I read them and this is one of them. Sarah giggles when she hears that she'll have a baby, but when the angel asks her why she laughed she says, "I didn't." The angel replies, "No, but you did laugh." Note to self: lying to the God of the

CALLED

universe is probably not an effective life strategy. Exactly as the angels predicted, Sarah delivers a healthy baby boy several months later and names him Isaac, which means (you guessed it), "laughter."

One day while Isaac is still an infant, Sarah finds Ishmael making fun of him and it doesn't sit well with her. Now that she's got her own son, Hagar and her kid aren't so useful anymore, so Sarah has them sent away.

Remember I told you this story related to the news you might watch tonight? Let me lay down a piece of information to put it into context. Ishmael is the father of the Arab people, and Isaac is the father of the Jews. You know, the two people groups that still despise each other and battle over everything from land rights to religion? Yeah, them.

I feel a little sheepish saying this, but I'll just throw it out there. When I understand things like this, a voice in the back of my head whispers, "Wait, so this stuff is REAL?" But yes, the anger and hatred between these two groups of people originated with one father and two mothers thousands of years ago.

Admit it. It's a little fascinating, hmm?

THE SACRIFICE OF ISAAC

After Hagar and Ishmael are sent away, things are quiet for a little while. The next time Isaac's name is mentioned, it's in a doozy of a story:

> After these things God tested Abraham and said
> to him, "Abraham!" And he said, "Here I am."
> He said, "Take your son, your only son Isaac,
> whom you love, and go to the land of Moriah,
> and offer him there as a burnt offering on one
> of the mountains of which I shall tell you."
> GENESIS 22:1-2

Let's call this what it is: the perfect follow-up to the circumcision talk.

"You know that son I promised? The one I said was going to father many generations? The one you love? Yeah, him. Now I need you to go ahead and start walking in this direction, and then I'll tell you exactly where to go. Once you get to that spot, you're going to kill him."

Well, that's sure not ideal.

✳ *Let's back up a bit, because this is important. What word did Genesis 22:1 use to describe what God is doing to Abraham? He _____ him.*

In case an alarm is going off in your mind right now because you thought God didn't test people, let's take a minute to clarify something.

Does God test us? Yep. He sure does. Does He tempt us? No, He doesn't.

Is there a difference? Yes, and it's one I would love to go into more detail on, but for now let me just try and make it a little more clear.

God tested Abraham (and tests us) because He knows we can (and hopefully will) make the choice that reflects our trust and love for Him. He both sets us up to honor Him and He strengthens us in obedience.

Tempting someone is more like inviting them into a situation where you want them to fail. If you're watching what you eat and I start waving a candy bar in front of you, that's tempting; I'm deliberately setting you up. God doesn't set us up. Satan, our adversary, does.

That said, testing isn't easy, and this is a great example. God basically asked Abraham to perform a human sacrifice, never condoned before, and God also seems to be eliminating the outcome He has promised—children coming from Isaac. Quite frankly, it seems like a pretty intense way of assessing someone's loyalty.

But Abraham knows something we also need to understand—the character of God. So Abraham wakes up early, saddles his donkey, packs everything they'll need, rounds up some servants, and heads out in the direction the Lord has told him to go.

✳ *In Genesis 22:1, what does Abraham say in response to being called by God?*

Hear me say this: He is obedient to a situation that doesn't make sense to him because he trusts God more than what he can see with his own eyes.

Lemme just add that to my Pinterest board real quick, because I can use the reminder.

Abraham gets to the mountain, and God shows him the exact place to slaughter his son. Abraham binds Isaac up and raises his knife in the air to kill him, but at that very moment, God calls to Abraham.

✳ *What is Abraham's response to God saying his name? (v. 11)*

CALLED

Abraham's really good at telling God he's on board, isn't he?

Have no fear. This one doesn't have a sad ending.

✳ *Read what happens in Genesis 22:12-14.*

Why? Why would a loving and kind God ask a man to kill his own son?

That leads to another question. Why would God sacrifice His only Son, His only begotten Son, whom He loves?

This is the first time the word *love* is used in Scripture, and it's to describe the love a father has for his son.

We're transitioning to Jesus right here in case you didn't pick up on that.

Isaac had to carry his own wood up the mountain on his back until he came to the place of sacrifice. Sound familiar? It should. Because approximately 2,000 years later, another man would do the same. In fact, He would do it on the same mountain range.

God would sacrifice His only begotten Son—the Son He loves—for a world of people who have made a habit of turning their backs on Him.

Did Abraham believe he was going to have to kill his son? Yes. Based on Hebrews 11:19 (Go ahead and look it up. I'll wait here. And there's no shame in using the table of contents), yes, Abraham believed it. But I also believe he put stock in the reality of the situation, which was this: he knew he served a trustworthy God.

As the story ends, we see Isaac and his father coming back down the mountain together.

✳ *What does Abraham call that place? (Genesis 22:14.)*

And indeed, He would.

But I'm getting ahead of myself, and I don't want to do that.

Let's call it a day and meet up again tomorrow. We've got miles to go, friend, but you've already covered more than you think you have.

Sleep well, because tomorrow we're going to hang with a mister who majored in deception and went on to become one of the most important people in the pages of the Bible.

I love a good story. Don't you? (Again … rhetorical. But I sure hope you said yes.)

DAY 3
REBEKAH, ESAU, & JACOB

Let's fast-forward a few years. Sarah has died, but Abraham (who is now older than he was in the last section, which is really, really, really old), is still kicking.

He wants to make sure that his son Isaac has a wife before he dies, and he sends his servant to find him one. But there's a catch. Read Genesis 24:1-4.

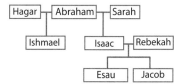

* *Where did Abraham want his servant to find a wife for Isaac?*

Can you picture this on the map? If not, take a glance back to page 38 and find Haran.

Through a providential encounter Abraham's servant finds the woman God has chosen to be Isaac's bride. The servant receives her family's blessing, and begins the trek back to Canaan. Isaac is instantly smitten with Rebekah, and she is great comfort to him as he mourns the death of his mother.

Eventually, Rebekah becomes pregnant with twins. She can feel them jostling in her womb as if they are constantly fighting.

* *When she asks the Lord why this is the case, what does He tell her? (Genesis 25:23)*

Esau was born first. He was red-headed and very hairy. His brother is born right after him, but it seems that wasn't the order he was hoping for. Jacob is delivered with his hand holding Esau's heel, as if he was trying to hold him back.

Incidentally, names always have meaning in Scripture, and Jacob's means (you guessed it), "heel-grabber." It also means "deceiver," which he'll grow into by and by.

Jacob was a mama's boy; quiet, reserved, and not really great at manly stuff. Esau, on the other hand, was a fantastic hunter and loved all things outdoorsy. One day, Esau comes home from hunting and he's famished, so Jacob offered him some stew. Unfortunately for the impulsive Esau, this meal came with a high price. Read what that was in Genesis 25:29-34.

 RENAMED

* *What did Esau give Jacob in exchange for some stew?*

Not his finest moment, eh? As the firstborn, Esau received the birthright, which, according to custom, meant he would receive twice as much inheritance as Isaac's other children. Because Isaac was a very wealthy man, this was no small matter. But it gets worse. The firstborn also typically received a blessing as well. The blessing designated who would become the head of the household after the father died, and because Esau was the oldest, it should have gone to him.

Remember sweet mama Rebekah? She's got some plans.

She wants her favorite son Jacob to get the blessing, so she concocts a plan to make that happen. She straps some goatskin on Jacob's arms (haven't we all?), cooks up a delicious meal, and makes sure Jacob is dressed in Esau's clothes.

Her hubby Isaac is in failing heath and his eyesight is terrible, so she sends Jacob in to trick him. Thanks, wifey.

* *Read Genesis 27:18-29 to see what happens.*

So now, Jacob has the blessing instead of Esau, and it can't be taken back. Once the blessing was given, that was it. Of course, Esau is beyond furious when he finds out what's happened, and Rebekah tells Jacob he had better flee before his angry brother kills him.

Sometimes I feel like a rotten mother and wife and then I think of stories like this and I think to myself, "Well, at least I've never glued fake hair on someone to take advantage of my dying spouse."

Jacob? You might want to run. Now. He does and has a dream.

* *What was the gist of Jacob's dream? (Genesis 28:10-15)*

Does this strike you as odd? Here we have a man who has manipulated those around him since (literally) the day he was born, and God is promising that all these amazing things are going to come from him? Remember, God made a covenant with Abraham, and He intends to see it through no matter what.

But that's not to say it's going to be all sunshine and roses, and this next story is a great example of that. Of all the stories in the Bible, this is

RENAMED

the one my kids want me to read to them the most—it's nothing short of an Oscar-worthy plot.

JACOB, LEAH, & RACHEL

Jacob is heading toward Haran to find his mother's brother Laban in the hopes that he will provide a place for him and protect him from his brother's wrath. As luck (joking, joking) would have it, he meets some men who happen to work for Laban, and as soon as they begin to speak, Laban's daughter Rachel wanders over.

Rachel	Jacob	Leah

Well, suffice it to say, Jacob is smitten. Rachel is spectacularly beautiful and all he can think of is marrying her. He goes to Uncle Laban and agrees to work for him for seven years in exchange for his daughter. After seven years, the wedding day finally comes, and possibly due to some bad lighting and a little booze, Jacob gets the surprise of his life the next morning.

✳ *What does Laban do? (Genesis 29:21-25)*

So the trickster got tricked.

And now he's married to the older, and evidently less attractive, sister and not his beloved Rachel.

✳ *He confronts Laban and Laban agrees to give him Rachel as well in exchange for what? (Genesis 29:27)*

He's hopelessly in love and agrees to the terms, marrying Rachel and beginning the second half of his "work-for-wives" program with Laban.

Awkward.

Leah, who is by all accounts a wonderful woman, is basically chopped liver next to Rachel. There's no question whom his favorite is, but there's one little thing that Leah has that Rachel doesn't seem to:

The ability to have children.

1.

2.

3.

✳ *Why did God allow Leah to have children? (Genesis 29:31)*

✳ *Continue reading through verse 35. In the margin record the names of Leah's children as well as the meaning of those names.*

4.

 RENAMED

I don't want you to miss something spectacular here. We're going to get into some more detail, but for now just note the meaning of her fourth son's name, and how it's different from the first three.

Judah would eventually become the father of many generations of great men and one great Man in particular: Jesus Christ. Isn't that beautiful?

Now let's see how Rachel is doing with all this baby fever. Read Genesis 30:1 and pat yourself on the back if you've never shouted the same sentence. It's a little dramatic, yes? Oh, Rachel ...

But Jacob takes care of the problem by having sex with her maid-servant (thanks, Jake) and providing a baby that will now be considered hers. This happens twice before Leah decides two can play this game, and she brings her maidservant into the picture too. Jacob has a couple sons with her as well.

Then Leah gets pregnant a few more times and provides him with more sons. And just when we get the feeling that old Jacob might need a nap, something really unexpected happens. Jump over to Genesis 30:22 to see what it is.

* *What happened?*

Now, remember, Rachel is the wife Jacob has loved from the moment he laid eyes on her. She is everything to him. And this is the only child they have together (at this point in the story). So it will come as no surprise to you that Joseph is now Jacob's favorite.

Isn't that an interesting frame of reference? Even if you've heard the story of Joseph, I wonder if you realized the reason he was so special to Jacob. Well, now you know.

And that's not all. Trust me, the dysfunctional family train still has a lot more stops.

At this point, Jacob is ready to move away from Laban, and he goes to him to ask permission to hit the road. It doesn't really go all that well, so Jacob ends up fleeing with his wives and children. As they travel, Jacob receives word that someone is headed his way, and it's not someone he's super eager to bump into.

* *Who is it? (Genesis 32:6)*

Jacob is terrified. He instructs the people with him to split into a couple camps in an effort to at least protect half of them. At one point he tells

his wives and children to go on ahead of him, and this is where we find a famously intriguing encounter that will forever change Jacob.

I'm getting goose bumps thinking about it, and I'm not even kidding. When you dig into the Word and invest in understanding it, you'll begin to feel the weight of certain stories differently. This is one of them.

Jacob, alone for the moment, encounters a stranger with whom he wrestles until the break of day. Read it for yourself in Genesis 32:22-32.

* *What did Jacob tell the man? (v. 26)*

* *What was the stranger's response?*

* *With whom has Jacob wrestled?*

God Himself wrestled with Jacob, the heel-grabbing manipulator. Only, God didn't leave him the way He found him, did He? God changed Jacob's name to Israel and left him with a permanent limp to remember this night.

Israel—the one who contended with God and prevailed.

Here is what God was saying to him: "You are no longer that person you were. There is no need for you to trick and grab and twist everything you can't make sense of. You are Mine, and you will have a legacy as powerful as any. Say goodbye to what you were, because it's gone."

God is still in this business, you know.

He loves to take the broken and weak things of the world and make them beautiful for His glory. Let's take just a moment as we close out this day and reflect on what a powerful gift this is.

* *What is one name you think of when talking about yourself? (Maybe it's adulterer, liar, addict, or bitter.) What is a name you pray could replace it? Whatever it is, remember this: your reputation is not the same as your legacy. Spend a few minutes praying and writing in the margin about the names you want to change, and the names you would rather claim as your own.*

NAMES YOU'D RATHER CHANGE:

NAMES YOU'D RATHER CLAIM:

RENAMED

DAY 4
FROM JACOB TO ISRAEL

I so wish I could be sitting with you right this minute, chatting over what we've covered so far. If I were, I would make sure to get your attention, and I'd probably have tears in my eyes at this point. I know that sounds silly, but the truth is that all of these stories—they aren't just black words on white paper. They're the backbone of the faith we can now claim as our own. These are real people God hand-selected to be a part of the lineage that will lead to the Messiah, Jesus.

We've just learned about the wrestling match between Jacob and God, and the spectacular moment when he received a new name. It's a name with significance to say the least—Israel.

But Israel still has to face his brother, and he has no reason to believe this meeting will go well.

✳ *Read Genesis 33:1-4. How does Esau respond to seeing Jacob?*

Crisis averted.

✳ *Where does God tell Jacob to take his family? (Genesis 35:1)*

Let's take ownership of our knowledge here, and repeat after me: "We are *not afraid of the maps.*" Mark the route Jacob took on the map on page 53.

1. They started in Haran (also called Paddan-aram) in Laban's territory.
2. Then they fled and headed toward Canaan (Genesis 31:18).
3. Jacob wrestled with God in Penuel (Genesis 32:30).
4. They got safely to Shechem (Genesis 33:18).
5. God told them to go to Bethel (Genesis 35:1), which is where Jacob had first received God's promise in the form of a vision (Genesis 28:19).

HELLO RENAMED   HELLO   12 $ ▲▲

OK, back to Jacob and the crew. They're obeying God and heading from Bethel to Ephrath, later known as Bethlehem, (these people move more than anyone I know) when something dramatic happens.

* *Read Genesis 35:16-20 and record the two major events that happen simultaneously.*

Let's take a teeny break for a minute. I wonder if you're doing this work, reading the verses, and still wondering when this is going to go somewhere. Because as far as you can see, these are just names of people that don't mean a lick to you. Maybe not, but in the event that you do feel that way, I want to have a chit-chat before we move on.

Every one of these names is important, and will shape your understanding of the entire scope of Scripture. Not just that, but your understanding of Christianity today. I know, it sounds like a big claim, but it's true. One day a few weeks from now you're going to be reading passages in the New Testament and a huge smile is going to spread across your face because they finally make sense in context. Pinky promise. So stay tuned and do your work—it'll be worth it.

Now back to business.

Hopefully that pep-talk geared you up for your last exercise of the day, because it's a big one. You're going to fill out the names of all of Jacob's (now called Israel) sons. Ready?

* *Read Genesis 35:23-26 and fill this in:*

Leah's sons:

1.

2.

3.

4.

5.

6.

Rachel's sons:
1.
2.

Bilhah's sons (Rachel's maidservant):
1.
2.

Zilpah's sons (Leah's maidservant):
1.
2.

That's a total of twelve, and these twelve are considered the 12 tribes of Israel (kind of—I'll explain that in a minute). Why? Because they are the 12 children of the man named Israel. Forgive me if that's obvious, but it wasn't always the case for me.

Now stick with me for a second, because this is going to get a little tricky. Each of these fellas is going to father a tribe that will in turn get a plot of land, but the breakdown looks a bit different from the list above and I want you to understand why.

Levi's tribe will be the priests, and they aren't going to get land, because the Lord Himself is considered their "land." So that means only 11 get land.

But wait! There's more.

Remember Joseph, who was Jacob's favorite? He's not going to get land either, but it's not because he isn't special. It's because he was so special that each of his sons (Manasseh and Ephraim) will get their own land. So in a sense, he doubled up.

When we take away Levi and Joseph from the mix, but add Manasseh and Ephraim, we get back to our total of 12. The lists vary a little depending on which book of the Bible you're reading, but they always work out to 12. It's not urgently important that you understand the details of the breakdown, but when you see what looks like a discrepancy from one book to another (Deuteronomy, Genesis), this is the reason for the difference. Good? Good.

Next up? The golden boy, Joseph.

12 TWELVE TRIBES

DAY 5
JOSEPH

OK, so you might have heard the story of Joseph and his rainbow-colored robe, but do you understand why that was important? Say no. Please say no. Because I want this to be an ah-ha day for you.

We know Joseph was Jacob's favorite, and so did everyone else, including his bitter brothers. In fairness, Joseph didn't play it down very well. He actually made a point of reminding them how special he was. His dad gave him a robe of many colors to signify his importance, and Joseph strutted around his brothers while wearing it and declaring his position in the family.

* *Read Genesis 37:1-11 and record the gist of what Joseph told his brothers about his dreams.*

They're over him. Really over him. So they do what any of us would do with our dreamy, prideful sibling: they ripped off his robe and threw him in a dry well to die. Then they decided to sell him into slavery to the Ishmaelites. (Hmm… where have we heard that name? Yep. These are the descendants of Ishmael, our favorite wild donkey of a man.)

For dramatic effect, they slaughter a goat and dip the robe in its blood to show their father to convince him that Joseph has been killed by wild animals. Needless to say, this moment probably didn't make it into the family scrapbook.

Obviously, Jacob is devastated that now he has lost his favorite wife and his favorite son, and he goes into a period of mourning where no one can comfort him. Little does he know that God has a huge surprise for him a few years down the road.

Joseph's captors take him to Egypt and sell him as a slave (boo). His owner (Potiphar) comes to depend on Joseph (yay!), but then Potiphar's wife falsely accuses him of rape (boo). Joseph is thrown in prison for his "crime" (boo) where he interprets dreams for prisoners and eventually for Pharaoh. Joseph lands in the good graces of the ruler (yay!). It's a roller coaster for sure, but it ends with Joseph as second-in-command over all of Egypt (yay!).

HELLO 12 $ SOLD

The dream Joseph had interpreted for Pharaoh involved telling him that Egypt was going to have plenty of food for the next seven years, followed by seven years of famine. He warned Pharaoh to stock up while he could, and Pharaoh listened. When the famine came, Egypt had more food than they needed, but the surrounding areas were suffering terribly.

And here's where the story takes a dramatic turn.

* *Who shows up in Egypt? (Genesis 42:6-8)*

* *Well, not all of them. Which one is missing from the crew and what does Joseph tell them to do? (Genesis 42:20)*

* *Look back at the lists you made of Israel's 12 sons. What insight does it give you into Joseph's request?*

The boys head back home and tell Israel they're going to need to bring Ben back to Egypt with them. Daddy's not happy about it, but concedes and sends them on their way.

* *Who does Joseph ask them about in Genesis 43:26-31?*

* *What brings Joseph to tears?*

Up until this point, the brothers really don't understand why they've been brought into the palace and treated so well. I imagine them shooting one another glances while they feast, wondering what brought about this amazing opportunity.

Eventually, Joseph reveals himself to them. Read all of Genesis 45 for yourself, because it's spectacular on so many levels.

EGYPT

* *Make any notes that come to mind when you read this.*
Did anything surprise you? Inspire you? Give you any
new insights into the story?

I love how tender Joseph is in these paragraphs, and the way you can see the little boy in him. He wants to see his dad and to reassure his brothers that all is well and God has had His way. He doesn't waste a moment by letting them stew in regret; he simply says that God prevailed over their evil intentions.

Well, that'll preach.

Jacob and Joseph are reunited and Pharaoh blesses Jacob. They are given the best of the land and ensured plenty of food and goodness, and all is well.

* *Read Genesis 47:29-31. What is Jacob's dying request?*

Egypt is not his homeland; Canaan is.

In Genesis 49, Jacob blesses all of his sons and prophesies what their lives and legacies will hold.

* *Read Genesis 49:28-33 and record what you learn about*
the specific place where Jacob will be buried.

DID YOU CATCH
THAT HAND UNDER
MY THIGH THING?
A STRANGE WAY
TO MAKE A PLEDGE,
ISN'T IT? I THINK
I'LL STICK WITH
PINKY PROMISE.

He wants to go home. Abraham's home. Sarah's home. Isaac and Rebekah's home. Leah's home. He wants to be gathered with his people in death, and Joseph honors his request. He and all of his brothers carry the body of their father and lay him to rest in the same cave as his ancestors.

Now that Jacob is gone, Joseph's brothers wonder if he'll turn his back on them—or worse. Read Genesis 50:19-21 to find out.

The Book of Genesis ends with the death of Joseph.

EGYPT

* *Read Genesis 50:22-26 and describe where Joseph was buried. Does this surprise you? Why or why not?*

Before we end this week's lesson, let's just take a minute for an overall recap. See how much of this you can fill in by memory and then look through your notes for the ones you can't recall. (Or you can check Genesis 35:23-26; 41:45-46; Matthew 1:2)

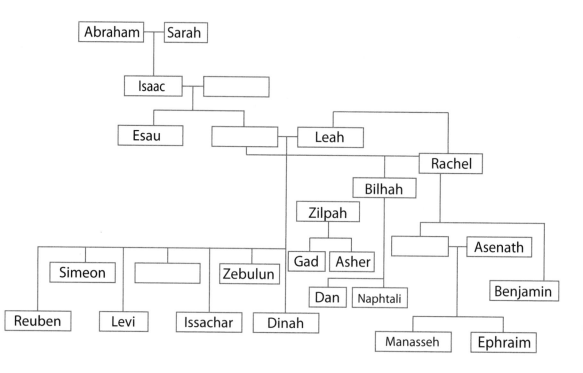

 EGYPT

FUN FACT:

HERE'S A FUN FACT JUST BECAUSE IT AMUSES ME. DID YOU EVER HEAR OF THE HYKSOS? I DIDN'T THINK SO.

Well, though the archaeologist-types argue over every detail, here's the broad strokes of the story. The three sons of Noah, Shem, Ham, and Japheth (Genesis 9:18) became the fathers of three extended families of the human race. The children of Shem are known as Semites. Who would have thought? The descendants of Ham—the Hamitic peoples. And the descendants of Japheth? The Aryans. What is that about?

The Semitic people include the Hebrews, the Arabs, and many other groups. The Hamitic people included the Egyptians.

Enter the Hyksos. The long and the short of it is the Hyksos were Semitic people who conquered Egypt in the 18th century B.C. They introduced the horse and chariot to Egypt. Then about 1521 B.C., according to the Encyclopedia Britannica, the Thebans (native Egyptians) rebelled and threw out the Semitic Hyksos.[1]

Why does that all matter? Well, Joseph went to Egypt during the Hyksos period. The pharaoh who promoted Joseph to second-in-command of all Egypt was a fellow Semite.

And 400 years later, when the Book of Exodus says, "a new ruler who had not known Joseph, came to power in Egypt." The ruler the Bible was talking about was an Egyptian who came to power after they threw out the Hyksos.

Is that fascinating, or what? I told you the Bible is talking about real people with real events in real history. Next time, maybe you'll believe me, and nobody needs to get hurt.

1. "Hyksos", *Encyclopædia Britannica Online*, s. v. [cited February 06, 2015]. Available from the Internet: *http://www.britannica.com/EBchecked/topic/279251/Hyksos.*

three

WEEK 3
EXODUS & THE PROMISED LAND

I have a method to my madness, I promise. What we've been studying for the past two weeks lays the foundation not only for the rest of the Bible, but also for understanding Judaism and Christianity.

Take a minute to review the icons you've studied so far. Remember what they represent?

Now, we turn our attention to the Book of Exodus and beyond. We get to join the Hebrew people, starting with a man God would use to change the course of history—Moses. We first find the Hebrews enslaved in Egypt and being treated terribly. The whip icon represents the Egyptian bondage. Apt and unfortunate I fear.

Next we see the stone tablets—the Law God gave Moses at Mount Sinai.

After the Hebrews attempt (and fail) to enter the promised land they wander in the desert for 40 years—hence the footprints.

Then (I'm not going to give away the whole story—you'll have to keep reading), the Israelites finally make it to the land God has promised them—gates anyone?

The last icon, the gavel, helps us remember the period of the judges. For a time longer than the United States has been a country, the Israelites lived as 12 separate tribes with no real central government. God gave them judges to rule for a few years at a time. At the end of the period of judges, we'll meet some kings, but first? We've got a sea and a lot of bridges to cross.

OPPRESSION   EXODUS   WANDERING   PROMISED LAND   JUDGES

SESSION 3: THE PATRIARCHS

REVIEW WEEK 2 HOMEWORK

* Day 1: What all did God call Abram to do, and what did God promise Abram that He (God) would do in response?

    • What's distinctive about a covenant anyway? Why is it so important?

* Day 2: What part of the whole parenting Isaac experience do you think would have been the most difficult for you? Why?

    a. believing God's promise though you had to wait for many years

    b. believing God's promise though you were way past childbearing years

    c. avoiding the temptation to try to control the situation, say maybe by getting a slave as a stand-in

    d. being willing to sacrifice the son for whom you'd waited so long

    e. something else

* Day 3: What did Jacob's name mean, and how did it accurately reflect his character?

    • Think of all that Jacob went through. In what events of his life do you see God working to change his character from a deceiver to a prince of God?

    • In what ways do you think the night spent wrestling with God (Genesis 32:22-32) changed Jacob's life?

    • In what sense was the event the climax of a long process?

    • How can you look back at your life and see God doing things to change your character?

* Day 4: What practical lessons do you think you can take away from the life and struggles of Jacob/Israel and his wives?

* Day 5: Even only children see something of sibling rivalry in those around them. What elements of Joseph and his brothers' lives made them the all-time case study for sibling rivalry—on steroids?

* Discuss the meaning of the first 10 pictures on the course map on page 177.

What aspect of Joseph's story impacts you most, and why? Some possibilities might include:

a. Joseph's faithful character enabling him to rise to power in Egypt despite the many betrayals he suffered.

b. God's providence—how He engineered the events to bring about the saving of His people.

c. The drama of the brothers' attempted murder, then sale, of Joseph?

d. The way Joseph served Potiphar, his fellow prisoners, and ultimately Pharaoh.

e. The emotional reunion of the brothers and then Joseph with his father.

f. Some other element of the story.

WATCH SESSION 3: THE PATRIARCHS (VIDEO RUN TIME 15:51)

DISCUSS

* You are not who you used to be. How has God changed you?

* How do real people from the Bible like Abraham, Sarah, or Jacob—people who made mistakes and manipulated situations—give you hope?

* How do fears of "getting what you deserve" hinder you?

* How are you encouraged to live differently because of what God has done for you?

Video sessions available for purchase
at *www.lifeway.com/seamless*

DAY 1
EXODUS

Week 3! Can you believe it? There's no time to waste so let's jump right into the second book of the Bible: Exodus. If you recall the end of last week's lesson, we had just said goodbye to old Joseph, whose body was buried in Egypt.

Like a beautiful tapestry, the Bible uses patterns of repeated events to signal really big moments in history. We see one with Moses: special circumstances around a child who will lead God's people.

* Isaac born to Sarah when she was far past menopause

* Moses miraculously saved from death as a baby

* Samuel's special birth ushering in the period of kings and prophets

* Isaiah predicting the virgin birth of One called "God with us"

* John the Baptist specially predicted and born to a barren mother

* Jesus, the ultimate miraculous birth, to save God's people

The people of Israel went to Egypt during the famine Joseph predicted, and now, many years later, they have become a threat to the Egyptians. The Israelites have grown in number and the Pharaoh fears they might gain too much power. He tells his people to treat them as slaves, ordering that they be mercilessly treated in an attempt to subdue them.

But it doesn't work, so Pharaoh comes up with a back-up plan. He tells the midwives they are to kill any baby boys born to the Israelites. The Hebrew girls are left alone.

* *How did the midwives respond to this decree? (Exodus 1:17)*

THE BIRTH OF MOSES

In chapter 2 of Exodus, we meet one of the heroes of the Bible. Read verses 1-10 and answer the following:

* *From which tribe did Moses' mother and father come?*

Maybe in the past you'd have had no context for what that meant, but now remember that Levi was one of Jacob's 12 sons, and the Levites were the priesthood of the nation of Israel. So instead of just glossing over this and storing it in your "another part of a verse that doesn't really make sense to me" category, I'm taking the opportunity to remind you that you already have a much better grip on the whole of Scripture than you think you do. We'll see these words repeat over and over as we go, and now you have tools to make sense of what you're reading.

As chapter 2 opens, a Hebrew woman (The genealogy reveals that her name was Jochebed. Any of those in your family?) has a baby boy.

OPPRESSION

* *Presumably, what do the midwives do when her son is born?*

* *And what does Jochebed do for the next few months?*

* *Eventually, this gets tricky and she knows she has to let him go. If the Egyptians come across him, it'll be dangerous not just for him but for their whole family. What does she do at this point?*

* *Providentially, he is rescued. Who rescues him and what is the unexpected result of it?*

So this is the second time we've seen this pattern of a Hebrew becoming part of the Egyptian Pharaoh's family. First with Joseph, and now with Moses. I could spend years studying the delicate twists and turns of Moses' life, but we don't have that luxury here. I'll do my best not to wander off too far from our path, but I want to point out something I think is a beautiful foreshadowing.

When Moses was born, he was supposed to be thrown in the water. He wasn't. When he was a few months old, his mother put him in the water and he was rescued. If you're keeping score, that's Moses: 2 and water: 0. Trust me, it's a pattern that will come to a powerful crescendo in a bit, when he ups the score a few more times.

MOSES: 2
WATER: 0

Moses grows up in Pharaoh's house, and eventually sees an Egyptian beating a Hebrew man. He becomes so enraged that he murders the Egyptian and buries him in the sand. Pharaoh hears about this and he's not too thrilled. He sets out to kill Moses but Moses flees.

I cannot make this point strongly enough. The Hebrew people—Abraham's descendants—are God's chosen people. They are the ones chosen by God to be in a covenant relationship, and for lack of a better word, they're just special to Him.

All throughout the Bible, we're going to follow this thread. God wants the Israelites (also called Hebrews and later called Jews) to love and serve Him, but God's people don't stay consistent in their

OPPRESSION

THE DESCENDANTS OF JACOB/ISRAEL WERE KNOWN AS HEBREWS. LATER IN THE EXILE TO BABYLON, THEY BECAME KNOWN AS THE JEWS. SO:

ISRAELITES =HEBREWS =JEWS.

affections. Over and over again He woos them to Himself, but the cycle continues. Keep that tucked in your mind while we read this next bit, knowing that we're going to get into more detail in coming days.

* *In light of that, read Exodus 2:23-25.*

I so hope you just read that and couldn't help but notice it made more sense than it might have a few weeks ago.

GOD CALLS MOSES

* *God's paying close attention to His people, and He's not missing a thing. He's setting the scene here for a rescue, and the call to lead that rescue comes to Moses in a rather strange way. Read Exodus 3:2 and record what happened.*

Have you wondered how the burning bush fit into everything? Well now you know. It's the place where God spoke to Moses and told him what He was planning to do with him. Moses responded to God by saying, "Here I am," (Exodus 3:4). He essentially said, "I'm ready and listening, Lord."

WHEN WE SEE SCRIPTURE USE THE PHRASE, "GOD REMEMBERED." IT DOESN'T MEAN HE FORGETS. IT MEANS, "HE ACTS."

* *God reminded Moses of an important fact. What did God say in Exodus 3:6?*
  "I am the God of your father, the God of _____, the God of _____, and the God of _____."

In the next few paragraphs, God tells Moses that He has better plans for His people than Egypt. He has a land set aside for them—the land He has promised—and it's almost time to go there. He tells Moses that he's the guy to bring them out of this horrible oppression and lead them to this amazing place, and Moses struggles to believe he's capable.

God gives Moses a helpful, yet not so exciting, tidbit: "You're going to ask Pharaoh to let the Israelites go, and he's going to refuse you."

Awesome. I'll just get right on that, then.

THE PLAGUES

Moses and his brother Aaron go to Pharaoh and just as God told them he would, Pharaoh refuses to release the Israelites. In response God sends a series of ten plagues to punish Pharaoh and the Egyptians. And

 OPPRESSION

listen—they aren't ideal. They include water turning to blood, frogs, gnats, flies, the death of livestock, boils, hail, locusts, and darkness. These aren't coincidental, by the way.

The Egyptians worshiped many "nature-gods," and each of the plagues was specific to those gods. For example, the Egyptians believed frogs were sacred and shouldn't be killed. They worshiped a frog-headed god that represented fertility. To remind them that He was the only God, Yahweh allowed thousands of frogs to die in their homes, the stench rising up like their false worship.

After nine plagues, Pharaoh still refused to let God's people leave the land, and Moses warned him of the final plague—the death of every firstborn child in Egypt.

THE PASSOVER

If you know anything at all about the death of Christ, you'll understand why I have tears in my eyes as I write this next part. Just before the last plague happens, God commands His people to take a lamb without blemish, kill it at twilight, and put some of its blood on the doorpost of their homes.

God explains that during the night He will "pass over" every house marked with blood, thereby protecting the firstborn children of His people. Tell me you see the beauty of this symbolism, because it isn't by accident. Jesus, referred to as the "spotless Lamb," will be sacrificed on our behalf, His blood protecting us from death.

From early in Scripture, we see the need for sacrifice. In all sorts of situations, an item was sacrificed on behalf of the people, thereby making it a substitution. Jesus Christ will serve as the ultimate Substitute and all of these beautiful images are leading up to that moment.

So we've traced the story from the beginning of time to a man named Moses—a man God will use to save His people and foreshadow His own coming—and all of it with this one simple goal: to rescue His beloved flock.

If you are a believer in Christ, close this book today with the knowledge that you, indeed, have been "passed over" because of the inexplicable, abounding love of a Savior who paid the highest price on your behalf.

If you have not yet become a follower of Jesus by placing your trust in Him, I would encourage you in two ways. First, maybe you could find a believer you respect and talk to him/her about having a relationship with Christ. Secondly, please do not give up on this

OPPRESSION

THE COVENANT NAME OF GOD:

have you wondered about the names *Jehovah* and *Yahweh*? They're both English equivalents of the name of God in the Old Testament. God's name was represented by the four Hebrew consonants *YHWH* (theologians call it the *tetragramaton*). Centuries ago English scholars thought it was pronounced *Jehovah*. Today most agree *Yahweh* more closely represents the covenant name of God.

study. The more you put the pieces together, the better I hope you'll understand and want to respond to Jesus.

The Bible is all about how Christ loves you personally, and wherever you are in your comprehension of that, I want you to feel welcome in these pages. Also, know that if you fall into the category of, "I'm not really sure what I think of this Bible thing," know that I'm praying specifically for you as I write these words. Thank you for the privilege of allowing me to be even a small part of your journey with Him.

OPPRESSION

DAY 2
THE WANDERING

In the last plague all the firstborn sons of Egypt die—save the ones from homes with the Passover blood—including Pharaoh's own child.

The devastated Pharaoh summons Moses and Aaron, tells them to get out of town and take their people and animals with them. The Israelites leave with God leading them with a pillar of cloud during the day and a pillar of fire at night. They follow, seeking the place God has for them.

* *Not too long after they leave, Pharaoh has a change of heart. What did he decide to do? (Exodus 14:5-9)*

The Egyptians get close. Very close. The Israelites see them, realize they are outnumbered and start to panic. With the Egyptians behind them and the sea in front of them, death seems certain.

The Israelites start shouting at Moses and Aaron, asking why they've done this to them. Remember the alternative is a lifetime of abuse and enslavement. But in their panic they want to go back.

Moses speaks these words, and they echo in my mind even today:

> "Fear not, stand firm, and see the salvation
> of the LORD, which he will work for you today.
> For the Egyptians whom you see today, you
> shall never see again. The LORD will fight
> for you, and you have only to be silent."
> **EXODUS 14:13-14**

EXODUS

On God's command, Moses raises his staff over the Red Sea, and the Lord sends a mighty east wind that blows all night turning the sea into dry land. The Israelites walk safely across as the water piles up to their right and left. When the Egyptian army follows, the raging sea swallows them.

Still keeping track? That's Moses: 3, water: 0.

 EXODUS

* *Read Exodus 14:30-31. How did the Israelites act when they got to the other side? Trust me, it's fleeting.*

THE TEN COMMANDMENTS

While Moses and Aaron are wandering with the Israelites, God gives them some helpful commands. His history with humanity thus far says we act pretty rotten, so God's going to lay out the ground rules on a pair of stone tablets and give them to Moses.

Let's take a moment to discuss the point of these rules, because a lot of people get confused about them. They think that to be a good Christian, you have to keep all of these commandments—always.

You respond, "That's impossible! The standard is too high! We could never do that!" And you're right.

So, did God set us up to fail? No. The purpose of the commandments wasn't (and isn't) that if we keep them all, we'll be good.

We can't be good. Not ever. Not the way God is good.

And that, my friend, is the point. He has to do it for us.

We're going to talk more about this, because laws will become one of the pivotal topics in Scripture, but for now I just want you to dog ear this conversation and know: while God gave us a standard for serving Him obediently, our salvation does not hang in the balance.

Reread that last sentence. And again if need be.

The point of the Law (not just the Ten Commandments, but a bunch more we're about to get into) is to show us how much we need Him.

So after God gives the Ten Commandments, He starts to lay down a TON of other rules. Rules about the altar, about restitution, about what we should eat and not eat, about sacrifices and the Sabbath and …

You get the point. It's a lot. The entire Book of Leviticus (yep, you can now check this one off too!) records all the laws God gave to the Israelites. For those of you who have attempted to read the Bible cover to cover, Leviticus is also known as, "I GIVE UP."

THE TABERNACLE

* *In the midst of all the law, God invites His people to do something. What did He tell them to make and why? (Exodus 25:8)*

WANDERING

God wants His people to make a temporary (Wait, why temporary? We'll get there.) home for Him so that He can dwell with them. For the sake of brevity, here is an illustration of what He was asking them to make.

He's not vague about instructions, either. Skim over Exodus 25-27 just to get a feel for how much detail He gave them.

* *Read Exodus 40. What separated the ark of the covenant from the rest of the tabernacle? (Exodus 40:3)*

Here's why that's important—I promise you'll understand why once we get to the end of this study together. The people are sinful, and in their sin, they cannot stand before a holy God. He is too perfect, too pure, and too wonderful. So, they are separated from His presence.

Once a year, the high priest would enter the holy of holies—the innermost part of the temple where the ark was kept. According to very specific instructions (I know you're dying to know, so you can read Leviticus 16 to satisfy your longing for detail), he would go in and make an offering on behalf of the people. (Read: substitution.) If he did anything wrong at all, the priest would die. No pressure. According to tradition, the people outside would tie a rope around the high priest's ankle so that in the unfortunate event that he made a mistake and dropped dead, they could drag him out. They weren't, after all, allowed to enter themselves, so this would be the only way to retrieve him.

Jewish people still celebrate the Day of Atonement, which they call "Yom Kippur." It is the holiest day of the year for them, and in keeping

□ EXODUS =
God rescues His people

□ LEVITICUS =
laws God gave the Israelites

WANDERING

with Jewish custom they will often fast and abstain from work. This is a time for them to reflect on their sins and to repent to God, praying for forgiveness.

＊ *Why do you suppose Christians don't celebrate Yom Kippur?*

Because we believe that Jesus the Messiah came in the flesh and offered Himself on our behalf, eliminating the need for any more sacrifice or intermediary intercession. Later, when we're in the New Testament, you'll see Jesus referred to as our High Priest. I hope that understanding the tabernacle and the Day of Atonement will help give you new eyes and comprehension once we get to those chapters, and that the words will hold new meaning for you.

So we've got the tabernacle all set up and we're traveling, traveling to the promised land. Let's jump back in and see what happens next.

THE ARK OF THE COVENANT REPRESENTED THE HOLY PRESENCE OF GOD. IT OCCUPIED THE HOLIEST PLACE IN THE TABERNACLE. IT WAS ALSO CALLED THE ARK OF THE TESTIMONY BECAUSE IT CONTAINED THE STONE TABLETS OF THE LAW.

DAY 3
TO THE PROMISED LAND

I feel like I'm talking a lot and you're being really quiet. It's one of the weird things about writing. You don't quite know when to pause and let the other person breathe or go get coffee. I'm assuming you'll just do that on your own, but as for now … chop-chop, we're back to the wilderness *(whomp-whomp)*.

THE WILDERNESS WANDERING

* *What did God promise Abraham would happen for 400 years? (Genesis 15:13-16)*

* *Exodus 12:40 says the Hebrews were in Egypt how long?*

In Genesis 15:16, God told Abraham his descendants would return to the promised land in the fourth generation.[1] Now read Exodus 16:35.

* *Do you see the pieces starting to come together a little bit? Take just a few minutes and jot down in the margin anything that stands out so far in what you've learned.*

So the Israelites wander in the wilderness for 40 years on their way to the promised land. They flip flop between being disappointed and disbelieving in God. "We want food. We're thirsty. Now we're sick of this bread and we want some good food like we had back in Egypt."

It's like a four-decade-long version of our family road trips.

God provides, they're grateful for a while, and then they get annoyed about something else and decide they aren't too impressed with God.

1. Kenneth A. Mathews, *The New American Commentary* (Nashville, TN: Broadman & Holman Publishers, 2005), 174-175.

WANDERING

* *Have you seen this pattern in your life or the life of someone you know?*

* *How has God provided for you? How have you forgotten His provision?*

This happens from Exodus 16–18, but now I want to show you a glimpse of something that might blow your mind a little. Is that dramatic? Too much build up? OK, then just leisurely find the Book of Numbers in your Bible and turn to chapter 11.

Skim over a few paragraphs. (Or, read it if you're an overachiever. There's room for you at this table, sister.)

Mind blown?!

Remember I told you one of the things that makes the Bible tricky to understand is the fact that it didn't happen chronologically the way the books appear? Well, here's another example. The good news for our purposes is that we just have to get a handle on where the crossover happens and different books of the Bible are talking about the same time period. So, get ready to understand the Book of Numbers. As if you didn't already. *Pshaw.*

The Book of Numbers is the story of the Israelites wandering in the wilderness for 40 years. It tells all about their grumbling, their sin, their rebellion, and lots of other happy thoughts.

It's two books further than where we are in Scripture, but that sentence tells us everything we need to know for our purposes. So when someone says, "Isn't that in the Book of Numbers?" (as they often do), you can access the part of your brain that says: "Numbers records the time period after the Exodus, before the Israelites had entered the promised land."

Boom. Done.

See? It's not so bad.

* *So wait … what group of people is the Book of Numbers talking about?*

WANDERING

* *Who is leading them?*

* *Where are they coming from and where are they going?*

* *How long are they wandering in the desert?*

Attagirl. And you didn't think you understood the Book of Numbers. Keep it up and you'll be spouting off lineage charts in your sleep. Well done, friend.

FIRST APPROACH TO THE PROMISED LAND

After traveling with the tabernacle for about a year, the Israelites come to the entrance of Canaan, the land God promised them. Moses sends 12 spies to check out the land and the people living there.

* *How long were the spies in the land? (Numbers 13:25)*

* *What does that number mean when we see it in the Bible?*

Ten of the spies say the people are huge and they can't defeat them. Bad choice. God said it was their land, right? Two of the spies say differently.

* *What are their names? (Numbers 13:30; 14:6)*

Needless to say, God is unhappy about all of this and He gets angry with the doubters. Moses intervenes on behalf of the people and urges God to reconsider. He reminds God of His character (which is always a smart negotiating tool), saying things like, "God, you are slow to anger and abounding in steadfast love, forgiving iniquity and transgression …" (see Numbers 14:18). Clever. I should have tried that with my parents.

☐ NUMBERS= time period after Exodus, before entry to the promised land

* *Read Numbers 14:26-30. Their disbelief is going to cost them severely. How is God going to punish the Israelites for doubting Him?*

* *But not everyone is included in the promised-land ban. Who, specifically, does God say will be allowed to enter? _____ and _____.*

PROMISED LAND

* *How long does God tell Moses the Israelites will be wandering in the desert and what rationale does He give for that number? (Numbers 14:34)*

God doesn't want this generation of people to enter His promised land because they are fickle and disbelieving. I'd love to call this anything but what it is: an accurate reminder of our natural posture toward God. We grumble, turn, and demand our own way. In response, our gracious God gives us life where we deserve death, but He also allows us to suffer consequences as a result of our disobedience.

So off they go to wander, and 40 long years pass. This generation dies out and the next takes over. Then it's time for round two.

They come back to the entrance of Canaan again. At the border Moses, who was not allowed to enter because of his own disobedience (Numbers 20:7-12), gives a series of final speeches. He tells his people to remember their God, the laws He has given, and to act in obedience. Moses knows he isn't going in, but he wants to leave a legacy with his beloved people. To do that he reminds them of the many times the Lord has interceded on their behalf.

Are you following? Picturing this in your mind's-eye? Good. Those speeches comprise the entire Book of Deuteronomy. Seriously.

Do you want to clap at all? Again, this is awkward because of the one-sided thing, but I hope you're starting to feel the power of understanding the story of the Bible. It's so, so beautiful.

I want you to write it down with me. Put pen to paper on your new knowledge—it's so much fun to gain a sense of the big picture.

* *Who is speaking in the Book of Deuteronomy?*

* *To whom is he speaking? (Think carefully. It's been 40 years, so they aren't the same people who were here last time. For a very specific answer, read Numbers 32:11-12.)*

* *Where are they geographically?*

 PROMISED LAND

In light of that, I want you to read Deuteronomy 1:6-8. Do you hear the faithful, impassioned voice of Moses saying, "You have stayed long enough at this mountain. … Go in and take possession of the land …"?

It's an encouragement to us as believers, isn't it? We can all stand to be reminded that when the Lord has promised us something, we hold fast to it regardless of circumstance and perceived ability.

In other words: the land is yours because I have promised it, not because you're capable of taking it over on your own. But we have to act in accordance with our belief, and as we all know, it's not always easy.

Gracious. It almost never is.

* *When have you been called to act on your beliefs, trusting in God's character more than your circumstances?*

* *What did you learn about God's promises through that experience?*

So our precious Moses is recalling everything the Israelites have been through and urging them to go forward in faith. He has to pass the baton. Who becomes the new leader of the Israelites? Before he dies, Moses hands over his leadership to someone special.

* *Who does Deuteronomy 31:7-8 name as the new Israelite leader?*

PROMISED LAND

Oh, my heart. I just picture Moses' shaky old voice as he gives his last words to the people he loves. It is the Lord Himself who goes before you.

Think about what we've learned together in the past few days about Moses—from his birth to the first time God told him He was going to use him. Think about the moment when Moses raised his arm and God parted the sea for God's people. Think of Moses' faithfulness in the wilderness. His life was one of the most powerful in all of Scripture, but it didn't end the way a traditional movie script would.

 DEUTERONOMY=
Moses' final speeches

Moses didn't enter the land that had been promised to the Israelites. So in effect, he did not get to realize the goal he had worked toward for a good portion of his life. When I first read this, it bothered me. I mean, he made one mistake. And that was enough to punish him like that? I don't know how I feel about that.

I had a turning point in my own faith as I wrestled with this. The Lord showed me something powerful I've leaned on many times in my life.

* *Read the 34th chapter of Deuteronomy and list anything that stands out as interesting or noteworthy to you.*
  Also, you might want to grab a tissue unless you're dead inside. Not that I'm judging.

God took Moses high up on a mountain and let him see the land, but God told him that he wouldn't enter it. To this day, nobody knows the place where Moses was buried, because God laid him to rest.

Can you imagine? God Himself buried His servant Moses. The tender care of a Father in this moment absolutely slays me every time.

* *Maybe you too feel like God brought you up to something you've wanted and worked for, but He didn't let you have it. Jot down your thoughts about the first disappointment that comes to your mind.*

I know I've struggled with this myself, and in my "perfect ending" scenario, life looked a lot different. But here's the part that makes me weepy: moments after Moses was blocked from the promised land, God brought him into an eternal life with his Father. The loss was momentary. Temporary. It paled in comparison to what was next.

Hear me say this, and let it bring you the peace you've been so desperate for. The same God who carried Moses to eternity will do the same for you as a believer in Christ.

It might not look this drastic for us, but the reality remains—life is a vapor. The disappointments that strangle us today will soon be forgotten, and even though His hands might not dig the dirt that lays us to rest, they will surely welcome us to heaven.

Who can understand a love like this? Not me.

Have courage, beloved; He walks before you always.

FUN FACT:

The first time the Israelites approached the promised land from the south desert. All they had to do was walk in. Forty years later they approached from the east and therefore had to cross the Jordan River at flood stage. Maybe life is easier when we obey God the first time.

GOD PENALIZED MOSES BECAUSE HE DISOBEYED GOD BY STRIKING THE ROCK WHEN GOD HAD TOLD HIM TO SPEAK TO IT (IN NUMBERS 20:7-11).

DAY 4
JOSHUA

Y'all, I'm still recovering from yesterday's lesson. I know you might think I'm a nut, and I'm not even saying you're wrong if you do. It's just easy for me to think of God as far away and unreachable sometimes, and when I read these accounts I'm challenged to remember He wasn't that way then and He isn't now.

God is intimately acquainted with all the details of our lives, and He works all things for the good of those who love Him (Romans 8:28). It's a good reminder, hmm? Back to Canaan.

ENTERING THE PROMISED LAND

Now that Moses is gone, the Lord speaks to Joshua, who will assume the position of leadership and bring the people into the land.

* *God is specific with Joshua about what is about to happen. Read Joshua 1:1-9 and describe what God tells him.*

We move to another of my favorite stories in Scripture (surely you're sensing a theme here)—the story of Rahab. Oh, Rahab—there are so many days when I thank God for choosing you to be a part of His story.

Joshua sends some spies into the land again (please don't say they're too scary … please don't say we'll lose … please be brave …) and they come to the home of a prostitute whose house is built into the wall that surrounds Jericho.

Wait. Jericho? I thought we were talking about Canaan. Where did that come from? No worries. Jericho is a city that is a part of Canaan.

* *Rahab agrees to hide the spies on her rooftop, and she lies to the authorities about it. Why does she take this risk? Read Joshua 2:8-11.*

PROMISED LAND

✳ *What does Rahab ask in return? (Joshua 2:12-14)*

She knows the Hebrews are God's people, and that He is going to be on their side. In exchange for Rahab's protection, the spies promise her that when the Israelites storm the land they will let her and her family live. But here's the catch: for the Israelites to know which house is hers, she needs to put a scarlet cord out the window to identify her location.

✳ *Does this remind you of anything we've talked about before? Like, you know, a time when something red was used for a similar purpose?*

☐ JOSHUA =
the Israelites enter
the promised land

If you didn't get it, the answer is "This reminds me of the Passover, when the Israelites had to put blood over their doors so they would be protected." You've got time before your group session. Just fill it in and we'll keep it between us.

The Israelites are ready to go in this time, but now they've got to cross over the Jordan River. That means holding the ark of the covenant way up high so it doesn't get wet. As the priests (quick—what tribe were they from? Good—the tribe of Levi.) start walking through the Jordan, God stops it from surging and allows His people to walk through.

I feel like God loves making water stop. Rank by rank, the whole army follows, and when the last soldier has set foot on dry ground, Joshua tells one member from each tribe to get a rock.

✳ *What does he instruct them to do and why? (Joshua 4:1-7) (Don't get overwhelmed by the details, just write down the primary reason he asks them to do this.)*

PROMISED
LAND

Throughout the Bible, we'll see people using stones to build memorials as gratitude for what God did for them in that place. Essentially they're saying, "Let's not forget God's faithfulness. Let's make a physical reminder for future generations that He didn't let us down."

So they've crossed over the river and entered the land, but they haven't taken possession of it yet. That will come through battle.

Remember this song? "Joshua fought the battle of Jericho, Jericho, Jericho ..." Yep. This is the Joshua and this is the Jericho. What happens next in the song? You got it! The walls come a-tumblin' down.

That's what happened. Joshua instructed his troops to march around the city for six days while blowing trumpets. On the seventh day they did it seven times, then shouted, (seven is always associated with perfection/completion in the Bible) and the walls fall down.

I love that Joshua is like, "Yeah. That sounds like a killer military strategy. Let's do this thing." I'm paraphrasing here.

He's seen what happens when they're disobedient. And I think once He knew what God wanted him to do, no matter how crazy it sounded, he knew it was the better alternative.

* *Have you ever felt God calling you to do something that seemed crazy?*

* *Did you do it? What were the results?*

Surprise, surprise. The walls fell down exactly as God said they would. The Israelites entered the land God had promised them. And they acted right and obeyed Him and always kept Him in mind for the rest of time.

That last part is totally not true. They're fickle, these folks ... can you imagine? For years they keep fighting people in Canaan to completely take over the land. Once they've pretty much gotten that under control,

  PROMISED LAND

it's time to divvy up the land. Each of the 12 tribes gets land (none for Levites and 2 for Joseph's sons, remember?).

Years pass. Things are relatively calm compared to what's about to happen, but before Joshua dies he reminds the people what God has required of them.

* *Read Joshua 23. List any commands that stand out to you.*

God is the only God. There is no other option. And if they start to believe differently, He will remove His hand of protection from them.

Just for fun, read Joshua 24:1-14. I know; that's not a sentence my ninth-grade self ever saw coming, but here's why I say it. I'm willing to bet that a few weeks ago you would have glossed over a bunch of this because it didn't make sense, and I want you to see how far you've come.

They aren't all unfamiliar names, are they? And you've got some context, which is always key when reading Scripture. Do you feel encouraged? I sure hope so—you should.

PROMISED LAND

DAY 5
THE JUDGES

When Joshua died, the Israelites had conquered most of the land but not all. This was a problem, because the Canaanites, who worshiped other gods, often led the Israelites astray.

＊ *Read Joshua 3:10. Which groups does God tell the people (through Joshua) they must drive out?*

Let's clarify this a bit. God tells them in no uncertain terms that all of the groups of people must be completely wiped out. He wants the Israelites to kill them. People who haven't studied Scripture much jump to stories like this and point an angry finger, claiming that God is cruel. Not so fast.

These groups of people were bad news. They've gotten so far away from God that they're participating in acts of bestiality and child sacrifice. God wants to protect His people from such horrifying conditions, so He gives them specific instructions. He doesn't say, "Go in there and rage against everyone. Kill everything you see." God tells them to drive out specific groups, because He knows their influence will be devastating to His people. But they don't exactly listen. And that's a problem, because now they've started to get friendly with these new neighbors. They're doing more than sharing morning coffee and extra tomatoes, too.

The Israelites start to worship the Canaanite gods. They intermarry. They decide that maybe God wasn't right about these people—they're perfectly wonderful. And the best part is, the Israelites remain free to worship their God because it's a free-for-all. I mean, just worship whomever you want! Join us on the mountain at 6 for refreshments and Baal worship. Bring your God and we'll all have a party together.

It's all so lovely, isn't it?

We laugh, but it's just like us. We know what we're commanded to do for the sake of the Lord, and yet, we often think, *they're just misunderstood. Maybe we should just cozy up here and live some life together.*

There you have it. God said He had already given them the land. Victory was as good as theirs. They just had to go on in and take it.

But they didn't. As you can imagine, this isn't what God had in mind and He takes action.

* *What will happen as a result of their disobedience?*
   (Judges 2:11-15)

JUDGES

God raises up judges to keep the people in check, but it's a Band-Aid®
on a ruptured artery. They just won't stay on the straight and narrow
with God. So they repeat the following cycle over and over:

First God raises up a judge. Then the people act right for a while
but when the judge dies they fall into rebellion and sin. Rebellion brings
punishment, usually by foreign oppressors. Finally, the people cry out
for mercy and the Lord gives them another judge to deliver them.

Have you ever struggled with an area of sin in your life, and when
you're in the pit of it you find yourself making all kinds of promises about
how you'll never do this again? And you mean it, but some time after,
you get lackadaisical and find yourself back there again, only to cry out
in desperation once you've hit bottom. That's what's happening on a
grand scale in Israel during this time. If you want to read more about the
different judges, you can find them in the Book of, umm … Judges.

A couple that might sound familiar (but that you possibly didn't
know were judges) are Gideon and Samson.

The period of the judges ends with Samuel, but before we talk about
his life, I have to pause and tell you a little about his early days. Things
always look different when you know the backstory, right?

Flip over to 1 Samuel and let's meet this little miracle.

* *Elkanah had two wives: Peninnah and Hannah. Peninnah*
   had children with him, but Hannah didn't, because, as
   1 Samuel 1:5 tells us, God had _____

   _____ _____.

I wonder if Hannah ever got to the end of her rope and shouted, "Sure,
I can't have a baby. But your name is still Peninnah!" It's just a thought.

Every year, they would go to a place called Shiloh to make their
annual sacrifice. One year while they're there, Hannah is in the temple
praying through her tears and she promises God that if He gives her a
son, she will give him back to the Lord.

Eli the priest is watching her, and he misunderstands, thinking she's
drunk. He rebukes Hannah, but she explains that she's really upset and
also, sober (*thankyouverymuch*).

A JUDGE WAS
A COMBINATION
MILITARY DELIVERER
AND CIVIL RULER. IN
THIS PERIOD
12 JUDGES DELIVERED
AND GOVERNED
ISRAEL:
1. OTHNIEL
2. EHUD
3. SHAMGAR
4. DEBORAH
5. GIDEON
6. TOLA
7. JAIR
8. JEPHTHAH
9. IBZAN
10. ELON
11. ABDON
12. SAMSON

*(some lists include Eli
and Samuel as judges)*

☐ JUDGES=
God gave the Israelites
judges to rule them

JUDGES

Eli blesses Hannah, not knowing how it will eventually bless him.

Hannah gets pregnant and gives birth to a son. When he is weaned, she brings him back to the temple at Shiloh, finds Eli the old priest and reminds him who she is. She explains that when she prayed for a son, she made a promise to God and now she's here to make good on it. She leaves Samuel in Eli's care to be raised in service with God.

Raise your hand if you're a parent and for one fleeting moment this actually seemed like a good option after a long day. I don't judge you, sister. (Judge. See what I did there?)

Eli has sons of his own, but they're rotten. Samuel isn't. One night Samuel has an interesting conversation.

* *In the margin describe the general story from 1 Samuel 3.*

Context, context, context! You've probably heard the verse, "Speak Lord, your servant is listening," but now you know who said it and why. God tells Samuel bad things are going to happen because of Eli's wicked sons. The presumption is that Eli wasn't doing much to make them shape up.

Samuel became both a prophet and the bridge between the period of Judges and the period of rule by kings. During this time, the Israelites and the Philistines battle and the Israelites lose because of how wicked Eli's sons were.

* *When Eli gets the news that the ark of the covenant has been stolen by the Philistines, he takes it pretty hard. What happens in 1 Samuel 4:18?*

Another life lesson right there. If you're old and heavy, don't hang out in a chair by a gate, because disaster might strike.

Just for kicks, read about Eli's daughter-in-law in verses 19-22.

"Hi. I'm Ichabod. My mom gave me that name after my wicked dad died, my grandpa tipped his chair and broke his neck, and the ark of the covenant was stolen. Let's hang out! I'm full of happy stories."

The Philistines don't keep the ark of the covenant for too long because terrible things start happening and they realize they might be messing with something they can't control. Suddenly it's not the lucky rabbit's foot they were hoping for and they get nervous.

Meanwhile, the Israelites are annoyed that all the other nations have kings, and they want one of their own. The whole point for the Israelites

JUDGES

was that God wanted to set them apart and make them different, but over and over again we see them wanting to be like everyone else.

Feel free to make any application to your life that you feel is appropriate. As for me, I simply can't relate.

* *In what ways are you called to be 'set apart' and different from the world? How have you succeeded? How have you failed? Respond in the margin.*

Samuel warned the Israelites that God was their King, and that the ramifications of a man ruling over them might not be as great as what they imagined. But they insisted. So God told Samuel to just give them what they wanted. Samuel has taken their rejection personally, and in one of his chats with God, he complains that his feelings are hurt.

* *How does God respond? (1 Samuel 8:7-8)*

This isn't about you, bud. It's about Him.

And unfortunately this is a lesson they're going to have to learn the hard way. We'll learn all about the kings in the next section.

Before we leave the time period of the judges, take a few minutes and read the story of a wonderful woman who will take her place in the history books. The Book of Ruth is short but beautiful, and I want to close out our time this week by asking you to read it in its entirety. I'm willing to bet that if you pay attention, you might just see the symbolism of a mighty Redeemer who is still yet to come.

* *You'll get a kick out of this, so I'll close with this. Look up Matthew 1:5. Who does it say was Boaz's mother?*

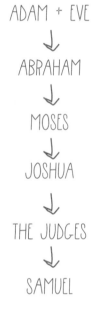

ADAM + EVE
↓
ABRAHAM
↓
MOSES
↓
JOSHUA
↓
THE JUDGES
↓
SAMUEL

☐ RUTH=
a story of redemption

Isn't that awesome? The woman who trusted the Israelites birthed a son who would marry a faithful woman and from their lineage would come Christ Himself. So the prostitute who was saved by a scarlet cord is one of Jesus' ancestors. The perfect, holy Messiah sent to save the world would be born into a family of scandalous repute, and His love for sinners wouldn't stop there.

JUDGES

four

WEEK 4
THE KINGDOMS & THE PROPHETS

Alright, ladies. We're digging in DEEP with this week's material. I used to be so confused about all the details of the kingdom, the kings, and the prophets, but now, it's all crystal clear and I rattle off battles in my sleep.

Well, either that or this is the week where my editor got sick of me saying, "Little help here?" at least 600 times. Graciously, he honored that request (Thank you, Dale).

I say all of this because, well, it's confusing. Lots going on. A lot of people talking to a lot of other people and a lot of shifting and moving and chocolate and pop tunes. OK, I admit some of those were coping mechanisms. Bear with me. We're going to get through this together. But don't get down on yourself if it takes you a few times to do so.

Naturally, our icons are going to come in handy again as we dive in. When you turn the page, you'll be learning about the United Kingdom. Well, not the "Duchess Kate" United Kingdom, but she would make an adorable icon as well. So think of her (and the Old Testament) when you see that little crown on the coming pages.

We'll see something very important this week—the temple. So the icon? I know, brilliant, wasn't it? And more than just a building … so much more. Stay tuned.

Next up? The broken crown. I bet you can imagine what that symbolizes, can't you? The Divided Kingdom. What? You have no idea what I'm talking about? No worries, pet. You will.

Then we'll find a lot of drama in the promised land, which will lead to the exile (see the arrows pointing out?) and the eventual return of a portion of God's chosen people (indicated by the last arrow, which kind of reminds me of the refresh button on my computer.)

The one I used 1,278,567 times in this week's lesson.

But who's counting? Oh wait…Dale is.

UNITED KINGDOM   TEMPLE   DIVIDED KINGDOM   EXILE   RETURN

SESSION 4: THE EXODUS AND THE PROMISED LAND

REVIEW WEEK 3 HOMEWORK.

* Day 1: Why in the world do you think, when God's people needed rescuing, He chose to send a baby (Moses)?

  • What part of the story of the life of Moses builds your faith? What part of the story surprises you? What part confuses you?

  • Has God ever rescued you in a way you would never have imagined? Or possibly in a way you didn't recognize as His deliverance until much later?

* Day 2: What did you learn about the origin and significance of Passover?

* Day 3: What purposes (you can certainly think of more than a few) did God have in giving His people ...

    • the Ten Commandments?
    • the tabernacle?
    • the ark of the covenant?

  • Why do you think God chose to have His people wander in the wilderness for 40 years?

* Day 4: How do you feel about the fact that Moses didn't get to go into the promised land with the people? (He did get to go later, though. See Matthew 17:1-5). What lessons do you think you could draw from the end of Moses' earthly life?

  • How does the red cord in the story of Rahab fit into the Bible story of redemption?

* Day 5: If God used special birth narratives to mark major turning points in Scripture, why do you think the birth of Samuel fits that list? What major change did Samuel signal?

  • In what ways are you called to be "set apart" and different from the world? How would you say that you have succeeded? How have you failed?

* Review and discuss the course map on page 177.

#seamlessbiblestudy

WATCH SESSION 4: THE EXODUS & THE PROMISED LAND (VIDEO RUN TIME: 16:51)

DISCUSS

* What are some situations or circumstances where you've doubted that God would come through for you? What caused your doubts?

* What hinders us from trusting that God is going to give us exactly what we need?

* The reward of Ruth's obedience was provision by her redeemer, Boaz. Compare and contrast the parallel in our relationship with Jesus.

DAY 1
KING SAUL

Big picture check in. We've watched the Israelites form as a nation and leave Egypt for the promised land. They've entered, divided up the land, and made progress in defeating the inhabitants. Unfortunately, they haven't conquered all of the people of the land and the remaining groups are a bad influence on the Hebrews. And the 12 tribes are just that—divided groups of people. No nation.

God wants the Israelites (and all of us) to be monotheistic, believing in and worshiping the one true God. The inhabitants of Canaan and surrounding areas are polytheistic, meaning they worship many gods.

The Israelites demand a king so they can be powerful and look to a man for leadership—which will inevitably lead them to look less at God. Samuel warns them that demanding a king is an awful decision, but the Israelites don't care.

So we meet the man who will become their first king, and the story starts out nicely. Saul is incredibly handsome, tall, and wealthy. When Samuel meets Saul, God confirms Saul's the guy who's going to be king, and Samuel passes along the message.

Saul doesn't go for it initially, and actually shows some humility, which will not be his trademark response for too long. Eventually, he accepts the role and is crowned king. For a few chapters, we'll see Saul as a victorious leader as he dominates many enemies in battle. Things are going swimmingly.

That is, until Saul disobeys Samuel's instructions about an offering. He acts out of his own will instead of God's command, and as a result, Samuel delivers a powerful blow in the form of a prophecy.

* *Describe what Samuel tells Saul will happen as a result of his actions (1 Samuel 13:13-14).*

Sorry, Saul. It's not looking good.

 UNITED KINGDOM

✳ *How does Samuel describe the man who will take Saul's place?*

Depending on the translation you are reading, you may have said "a man loyal to God" or "a man after God's own heart." Saul continues to make poor choices, and eventually God intervenes and tells Samuel to strip the kingdom from him. In part of Saul's apology to Samuel, he says these words, "I have sinned, for I have transgressed the commandment of the LORD and your words, because I feared the people and obeyed their voice" (1 Samuel 15:24).

    Well that'll sure get my attention. Not that I've ever made a bad choice because I was looking more to people than to God, because I would NEVER DO THAT (insert major irony here).

☐ **1 SAMUEL=** God gives His people a king

✳ *How about you? Do you ever let other people's opinions shape your actions? How does that work out for you?*

Typically, kings ruled until death and were replaced by a son, but in this case, God removed kingship from Saul's family because of his sin. We will get to meet Jonathan, Saul's son, a bit later, and he's a good warrior like his dad, but he won't ever be crowned king. Instead God tells Samuel to go to the house of Jesse because He has chosen one of Jesse's sons to be king.

✳ *What does Samuel think when he meets Jesse's son Eliab? (1 Samuel 16:6-7)*

✳ *Why does he think that and what does the Lord tell him in response?*

Samuel meets all the sons Jesse introduces, but God makes it clear to him that none of these fellas are the chosen king. Finally, Samuel asks Jesse if he has any other sons.

   UNITED KINGDOM

I smile when I think of Jesse's reply. I imagine him sheepishly answering, "Ummm, yeah. There's one more. Name's David, but he's not much of a warrior." He scans the selection of men he's already presented and finishes hesitantly.

"He's a shepherd boy, that one. Out in the fields tending to the livestock. But I can get him."

How many times have we seen this happen? Leave it to us to pay attention to the wrong attribute and jump to the wrong conclusions.

Jesse brings David to Samuel and the rest is history.

Samuel knows he has found his guy. It won't happen right away, but he has no question: David the shepherd will reign over Israel as king.

In the meantime, Saul has gone crazy. The Spirit of the Lord has left him and he has become a madman. His servants tell him they have a great idea: they'll bring in a musician. Harp music will calm Saul down. One of the servants knows of a young man particularly skilled with the harp, so Saul sends word to the boy's father to see if something can be arranged. Does anybody detect God at work here?

"Hey, Jesse? Yeah. King of Israel here. Listen … I've kind of, well … lost my mind and I need some music therapy. I hear you've got a guy."

* *Who does Jesse send to care for crazy Saul?*
(1 Samuel 16:19-20)

Well, isn't that just cozy? The nutcase has no idea that this little harp-boy is going to take his job. That surely would have put a damper on things.

Time passes. When next we see Saul, the Israelites have been fighting the Philistines. They've come up against a rather formidable foe, and one day when he's out looking for his strapping brothers, David happens upon the battle scene. He asks what's going on and the soldiers explain that they're trying to kill a giant named Goliath.

I have a feeling you might know where this is going.

David boldly says he'll have a go at this guy and Saul allows him to try because he seems so darned determined.

* *What happens? (1 Samuel 17:38-51)*

After this, Saul's son Jonathan and David become BFFs—and Saul turns green with envy because of all the attention focused on David. It's your classic, "Shepherd-harpist kills a giant and gains the love of the people" story, with a side order of jealous king thrown in for good measure.

Saul wants David dead.

Jonathan warns his buddy that homicidal dad is really ticked and suggests David escape. He flees, and spends more than a decade of his young adult years running from crazy king Saul. In the process David writes several of the Psalms.

Remember how I told you the Bible doesn't always list things in chronological order? Here is a great example. Go ahead and flip to Psalm 59 and read through it.

It has a lot of words, but I can summarize it for you: "Please don't let psycho-Saul and his army kill me."

Even though it might feel like we're moving slowly by the pages, the truth is we have covered a lot more than you realize. David wrote a good bit of the Book of Psalms, with several of them commemorating different events in his life. Eight Psalms discuss the time period when David was fleeing from Saul.

Saul is furious that David is still alive, and is desperate to reclaim power. In his rage, he decides to find a psychic (epically bad decision) to conjure up Samuel's spirit now that he's dead.

* *What does Samuel's spirit tell Saul is about to happen?*
  (1 Samuel 28:19)

Well, that's a downer.

These "summon the dead" parties never seem to go exactly right, do they?

Please note what Samuel says to Saul in 1 Samuel 28:15— "'Why have you disturbed me by bringing me up?'" Old and considerably dead prophets seem to be so easily annoyed. I mean, let him just be dead for goodness' sake.

As predicted, during battle the next day Saul receives word that his three eldest sons have been killed and he is warned that the Philistines are closing in on him. He doesn't want them to be the ones who take credit for his death, so he asks his assistant to kill him. Mr. Trusty refuses, so Saul ends his own life by falling on his sword.

And that brings us to the end of 1 Samuel. Now let's scoot into 2 Samuel, where we'll spend some time with one of the most important men in Scripture.

THE UNITED KINGDOM:

SAUL, DAVID, AND DAVID'S SON SOLOMON EACH RULED ABOUT 40 YEARS

SAUL WAS KING FROM ROUGHLY 1050 TO 1010 B.C

DAVID WAS KING FROM ROUGHLY 1010 TO 970 B.C.

SOLOMON WAS KING FROM ROUGHLY 970 TO 931 B.C.

☐ PSALMS= songs of worship expressing all types of emotion

   UNITED KINGDOM

DAY 2
KING DAVID

If we're making a short list of people you need to know from the Bible, here are the ones we've covered so far.

☐ 2 SAMUEL=
the kingdom of David

* *Put a check mark next to the ones you feel comfortable describing in a sentence or two. And maybe list a fun fact.*

☐ *Adam & Eve*

☐ *Noah*

☐ *Abraham*

☐ *Isaac*

☐ *Jacob*

☐ *Joseph*

☐ *Moses*

As a side note, the example above is certainly not intended to dismiss the role and importance of women in Scripture. I think as we get into the New Testament you'll understand why I chose to do things this way, but I certainly don't want you to think I'm ignoring the ladies.

I hope you checked all of those folks off, and if you didn't, you might want to glance over your notes before moving on. If you're feeling good about them, let's move on to King David.

Yes, he was just a shepherd boy to most people, and a wonderful harpist to others, but the truth of the matter is that he was hand-picked by God to play a pivotal role in the narrative of Scripture. God obviously loves the underdog, and we've already seen a bunch of examples that illustrate this point.

David's dad might have looked past him, but his Father never did.

The people love David, and after Saul dies, they make him king. At this point, Judah is on board (David is from the tribe of Judah, remember?) but the Northern tribes don't go for it for seven and a half

 UNITED KINGDOM

years. They pick one of Saul's sons to be their king, but eventually everyone becomes one big happy family—or at least one contentious nation.

Though we refer to the rules of Saul, David, and his son Solomon as the United Kingdom period, David was really the one to unite the tribes into a single nation. He captured Jerusalem and made it the capital, and then he uttered words from the most humble spirit: "See now, I dwell in a house made of cedar, but the ark of God dwells in a tent." (2 Samuel 7:2)

* *What do you think David meant by that?*

* *To whom was David speaking?*

For hundreds of years the Israelites had seen God as living in the tent called the tabernacle. David wants to build something permanent to house the ark of the covenant, and his friend Nathan prays about it, later confirming that God desires this structure to be built. In the same vision, God also tells Nathan to convey something else to David.

* *What did God promise regarding David and his family?*
(2 Samuel 7:8-17)

* *Now read David's response in 2 Samuel 7:18. How would you describe his posture before God?*

And this is where we have to draw a line in the lifetime of David. Second Samuel chapters 1–10 are all about his humility, his longing for God's righteousness, and his success as a leader. But in chapter 11, we see a shift that marks him forever. You may know the story, but go ahead and read 2 Samuel 11 to understand the context and timing of this event.

* *With whom did David have an affair?*

* *What did he do to try and cover his tracks?*

 UNITED KINGDOM

     ✳ *How did God respond to David's sin and deception?*

David's buddy Nathan confronts him in chapter 12, and David repents of his sin. He knows he has made a huge mistake before a holy God.

     ✳ *What does Nathan tell him will happen as a result of his sin? (2 Samuel 12:13-14)*

Forgive me for wandering a bit off topic for a moment, but I can't move on without doing so. Plenty of women reading these words will say something like this in their heads, *So my baby died (or some other tragedy happened) because I screwed up. It's my punishment. It's my fault.*

    I will be honest with you about something that is hard for me to understand; I believe that in this particular incident, David's son died as a result of his sin. The only reason I feel comfortable saying that is because the text is clear that this was the case.

    But that doesn't mean the same is true in any other instance. Unless you have been specially called of God to be king of Israel and to write a good portion of the Bible, hear me—or even better, hear God:

> He has not dealt with us as our sins deserve
> or repaid us according to our offenses.
> **PSALM 103:10, HCSB®**

I don't come to this story as a complete stranger; in fact, I have buried a child. So is that the case for me? For you? For the hundreds of people around us we watch go through horrible trials? Did our sin cause this?

    I believe it would be a ragingly irresponsible decision to think so.

     ✳ *Find John 9:1-3 and read it a few times. Let it soak in.*

Assuming causation in situations like these is one of the most dangerous things we can do—for ourselves and for others. I speak boldly here because I have been the victim of this kind of thinking, and I was wounded for quite some time. I would lay awake at night when we found out that Audrey wouldn't survive, recounting mistakes I had made in my life and camping out on the notion that I was being punished for my sin.

 UNITED KINGDOM

What I do know for certain is that God (as He did with Joseph, and with all of His people) will use the tragedies in my life for His—and my—ultimate good. That's not a trite answer; it's where I go to rest when I'm weary of the heartache.

This kind of reassurance can only come from prayer and genuine relationship with a God you believe is ultimately good, and I want you to know I understand if you struggle with it. I've been there, and I bet I'll be back in other moments.

But I do believe God is good, and like David, I want to be someone known for the way I love Him. As we close out today, spend a few minutes journaling what's going on in your mind as you process this story alongside your own.

* *Has there been a time when you felt punished by God? How has that affected your relationship with Him?*

* *As you finish journaling, read Psalm 51, which David wrote during his time of grieving.*

> DAVID WASN'T A MAN AFTER GOD'S OWN HEART BECAUSE DAVID DIDN'T SIN. HE WAS A MAN AFTER GOD'S OWN HEART BECAUSE HE KEPT COMING BACK TO GOD.

May God create in you a clean heart today, and renew a right spirit within you. Be reminded that He will never cast you from His presence, and ask Him to restore to you the joy of your salvation.

Praise His name, love. He is good.

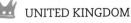

UNITED KINGDOM

DAY 3
THE TEMPLE

That was a hard day, wasn't it? Chapter 11 moments always are. But it's not the end of the story—not even close.

☐ 1 CHRONICLES=
religious history of
Israel at the time
of the kings

The Book of 2 Samuel covers the reign of David from start to finish, but guess what? (Get ready. Remember I told you this was going to happen?) *So does 1 Chronicles.* I know we aren't to that book yet, but chronologically, it's happening at the same time as 2 Samuel. The Old Testament has 6 history books. You can think of 1 & 2 Samuel and 1 & 2 Kings as one ongoing narrative. The two books of 1 & 2 Chronicles cover basically the same time period. The main difference is that Chronicles focuses on the religious history of the time period while the Books of Samuel and Kings focus on the political history.

☐ 2 CHRONICLES=
religious history of
Israel at the time
of the kings,
continued

We'll also see that the books of the prophets fit into the history, but let's not cause our brains to completely explode for the moment.

* *What happens in 2 Samuel 12:24?*

David's new son, Solomon, does not signal all good news, though. One of David's other sons (Absalom) tries to steal the throne from David and the king has to flee to escape being murdered by his own kid. A battle ensues and Absalom ends up dying, which devastates David despite the fact that Absalom was out to take David's kingdom from him.

David regains the throne but not a tranquil life. In one of the most difficult to understand episodes in the Old Testament, David angers God by performing a census of Israel (2 Samuel 24; 1 Chronicles 21).

* *What does David ask God to do in 2 Samuel 24:10,17?*

As punishment for David's action, God sends three days of pestilence on the land. To stop the plague, David goes to a man named Araunah and offers to buy his land to build a temple. Specifically, David wants to buy the threshing floor where farmers went to separate the edible part of grain from the inedible part. You might note that some Bible scholars say the threshing floor is used in Scripture as a symbol of judgment.

Araunah offers to give him the land, but David refuses, claiming that it must cost him something. In the end, David pays Araunah 50 shekels

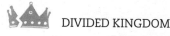 DIVIDED KINGDOM

(roughly $25,000). Although David had begun to plan for the great temple that would house the ark of the covenant, he wouldn't be the one to build it.

Before David dies, he passes on his advice to his son Solomon, who will take over his throne.

* *List the things David told Solomon in 1 Kings 2:1-4.*

Solomon began his reign much as his father had, with a desire to please and honor God. One night in a dream, the Lord told him to ask for anything he wanted and it would be given to him.

* *What did Solomon request? (1 Kings 3:7-9)*

Yay! Good job, Solomon. You could have asked for anything but you didn't. You are a shining example of all things good and godly.

For now.

Pleased with Solomon, God grants him tremendous wisdom. As he oversees the building of the temple, his reputation spreads far and wide. Solomon becomes the king with the most impressive brain and the most amazing structure people have ever seen. People seek him out to ask him questions about the meaning of life and they travel hundreds of miles to see the magnificent temple in all its splendor. Translation: Solomon is a hotshot.

Remember how the first 10 chapters of 2 Samuel told of David's success and chapter 11 started his downfall? The same story but a different book fits his kid.

* *The first 10 chapters of 1 Kings are an ode to Solomon's greatness. Find chapter 11 in your Bible and summarize the first sentence.*

Turns out Solomon (like his father) has a love for the ladies, and he takes many *(many)* wives. Some of them are from pagan cultures, and they lead him away from the one true God.

Needless to say, this does not go over well with God.

☐ 1 KINGS=
King Solomon

☐ 2 KINGS=
the various kings of Israel and Judah

☐ PROVERBS=
wise teachings largely from King Solomon

☐ ECCLESIASTES=
wisdom about life from a somewhat cynical viewpoint

☐ SONG OF SOLOMON=
a love poem between human lovers that illustrates how God loves His people

TEMPLE

Under the reign of Saul, David, and Solomon, the kingdom was united. But because of Solomon's sin, God is going to allow a split to happen after Solomon dies. The Northern Kingdom (consisting of 10 tribes) will be called Israel, and the Southern Kingdom (consisting of Judah and Benjamin) will be called Judah.

They will each have a series of kings ruling over them. Israel never had a good king and Judah only had a few. Overall it was a time of apostasy and chaos that lasted for hundreds of years.

UNITED
KINGDOM

ISRAEL   JUDAH

* *Read 1 Kings 15:29. Does that verse inspire you to become a king of Israel? I didn't think so.*

If you think I'm about to tell you who all of those people are, rest assured. I have no such intentions. For the purposes of this study, two things are important:

1. None of those names have made a list of popular baby names in my lifetime.
2. Life for the northern tribes (Israel) went on this way until they were conquered by the Assyrians (in 722 B.C. if you're keeping tabs).

The Assyrians deported the people of the Northern Kingdom of Israel and basically destroyed them as a people. Roughly 125 years later, the Babylonians conquered the Southern Kingdom of Judah as well. The difference was that after 70 years God brought the people of Judah back to reestablish the nation.

One of my life theories? It's always the Babylonians.

That's not true. I'm just trying to lighten the mood.

* *Here's a great bit of trivia for you. During the history of the Northern Kingdom they had 20 kings. In almost twice as long, the Southern Kingdom had the same number of kings. What does that many kings suggest to you about the success of rebelling against God?*

So … two tribes. North taken by Assyrians, South taken by Babylonians.

The latter happens in 2 Kings 25 (and 2 Chronicles 36:17-21), and it's a big deal. I don't throw out a lot of dates in this study, but here's one that matters.

Solomon's temple was destroyed by the Babylonians in 586 B.C.

 TEMPLE

* *Read 2 Chronicles 36:18-19. What did Nebuchadnezzar (the leader of the Babylonian army) do to Jerusalem?*

Make no mistake: this is a dark, dark moment in the history of God's people. They're taken from the land He promised them and held captive by their conquerors. Their grand temple, the dwelling place for the Word of God, has been leveled. Does this spell the end for our Hebrew friends? No, because:

* *How long were the Jews in exile? (2 Chronicles 36:21)*

We've covered a lot today. Next up? The Prophets.

FUN FACT: THE HEBREW BIBLE

THE BIBLE DIDN'T BEGIN AS ONE BOOK, BUT A LIBRARY. THOSE WHO PUT TOGETHER THE ENGLISH BIBLE ARRANGED IT, GENERALLY, IN CHRONOLOGICAL ORDER BUT BY TOPICS AS WELL. THE HEBREW BIBLE (OUR OLD TESTAMENT) IS DIVIDED DIFFERENTLY, IN THREE PARTS.

1. The Law (*Torah*)—the books of Moses: Genesis–Deuteronomy
2. The Prophets (*Nevi'im*)—which includes the historical books and what we call the prophets. The *Nevi'im* includes the former prophets, (Joshua, Judges, Samuel, Kings), the later prophets (major and minor prophets in the English Bible).
3. The Writings (*Ketuvim*)—the Psalms, Proverbs, Job, Song of Solomon, Ruth, Lamentations, Ecclesiastes, Esther, Daniel, Ezra, Nehemiah, Chronicles.

   With either organization, the Bible is really a complete library, inspired by God, telling the story of His revealing Himself to us over 2,500 years.

   TEMPLE

DAY 4
THE PROPHETS

Quick overview before we dive in today.

Under the leadership of Joshua, God's people took over the land He promised them. But they rebelled against Him over and over until He finally allowed them to be defeated and taken as slaves into foreign lands.

* *Try to fill in the following blanks from memory just to make sure you're getting the basics down.*

King David's son, _____ built the temple that housed the ark of the covenant.
Solomon sinned against God by taking _____ wives (and worshiping their gods). Because of this sin, the 12 tribes split into 2 nations. The 10 northern tribes were called _____ and the 2 southern tribes were called _____.
The northern tribes were defeated by the _____ and the southern tribes by the _____.
As a result, God's people were dispersed for _____ years.

Did you get all of them? Some of them? I hope so. If you want to check, I put my answers at the end of today's lesson along with answers to the next one, so don't hyperventilate with what I'm about to ask you to do.

We've covered 1 & 2 Samuel, 1 & 2 Kings, and 1 & 2 Chronicles in the past few days, and I want to make sure we're on the same page before we move on. So let me give you a friendly pop quiz and then a summary.

* *Label each of the following 6 descriptions with either 1 for Saul, 2 for David, or 3 for Solomon.*

___ *built the temple in Jerusalem*
___ *the first king of Israel*
___ *the man after God's own heart*

 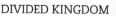 DIVIDED KINGDOM

___ the king renowned for his great wisdom

___ the king who began humble but ended up crazy

___ the king who conquered Jerusalem and united the country

This little section of history seems to be one of the trickiest for me to get straight, and it might be the case with you as well. So here's my summary in chart form.

1 SAMUEL	from the birth of Samuel to the death of Saul
2 SAMUEL	the actions of David as king
1 KINGS 1–11	the story of king Solomon
1 KINGS 12–2 KINGS	the 20 kings of Israel (Northern Kingdom) and the 20 kings of Judah (Southern Kingdom) Israel destroyed by Assyria
2 KINGS 17–25	Judah taken captive by Babylon

Is that as hard for you to get your head around as it is for me? Man, it's hard to keep all that history straight. Don't get stressed if it's still a little muddy in your mind—you'll get it. Reading the Bible just makes so much more sense when you have the broad outline of events in mind.

AFTER THE EXILE

After God's chosen people have been in captivity for 70 years, the king of Persia makes a life-changing proclamation.

✳ *What was the king's name? (2 Chronicles 36:22-23)*

✳ *What did he tell the Jews they were free to do?*

The first group of captives to return to Judah rebuilt the temple. The leader of that group was named Zerubbabel. Try saying that name three times real fast, but only if you have a tongue physician on speed dial. So this temple is often called Zerubbabel's temple. It wasn't as grand as the original, but they're making progress.

We need to back up a little and review to get this all in place. After Solomon's death the tribes split into the Northern and Southern kingdoms—

DIVIDED KINGDOM

UNITED KINGDOM

DIVIDED KINGDOM

ASSYRIANS
CONQUER ISRAEL

LAST YEARS OF THE
KINGDOM OF JUDAH

BABYLONIANS
CONQUER JUDAH

THE EXILE

THE POST-EXILIC
PERIOD

END OF THE OLD
TESTAMENT

the Divided Kingdom. That must mean that the time of David and Solomon was the United Kingdom 'cause they hadn't divided yet.

So we've got United Kingdom, then Divided Kingdom. Then the Northern Kingdom fell to the Assyrians, just leaving the Southerners, so let's call the next time the "Last Years of the Kingdom of Judah." The Babylonians conquered Judah and took them into exile, so let's call that the "Exile." After 70 years some of the exiles came back so we can call the result the "Post-Exilic period." (OK, I admit, I totally stole all these names, but they help us get it straight).

OK, we just put the 800 years from David to the end of the Old Testament in time periods we'll always remember, right?

Do you have any idea how much information you just absorbed? Wow. You can do this stuff. So where do the books of the prophets come in? During the time from the Divided Kingdom to the end of the Old Testament, God sent preachers called prophets to give messages to His people. Like a shuffled deck of cards, the 17 books of the prophets fit into the history we've been studying.

The first five (in the order they appear in Scripture, not necessarily chronologically) are Isaiah, Jeremiah, Lamentations, Ezekiel, and Daniel. They are called the "Major Prophets." The next 12: Hosea, Joel, Amos, Obadiah, Jonah, Micah, Nahum, Habakkuk, Zephaniah, Haggai, Zechariah, and Malachi are called the "Minor Prophets." Major and minor don't have anything to do with their importance, but simply the length of the books they wrote.

PROPHETS OF THE DIVIDED KINGDOM

Let's start with the prophets who spoke to Israel before they were defeated: Jonah, Amos, and Hosea. Jonah is a special case. He was probably the very first of the written prophets and the only foreign missionary in the Old Testament. He traveled to preach to the Assyrians. Amos and Hosea urged the Northern tribes to shape up, or face God's judgment. They didn't listen and, well, remember the Assyrians?

* *What do you think of the message God had Amos deliver to the people of Israel? (Amos 7:17)*

Alright, now on to Hosea. His story is fascinating. God told him to marry a prostitute named Gomer. After he married her, Gomer was continuously unfaithful to Hosea. She eventually ran off with other men and became a slave to them. Hosea finds her and buys her back, determined to love her well despite her actions.

Hosea's book is a sermon and his marriage is the sermon illustration. In one of the most beautiful pictures in the Bible, Hosea's love for Gomer shows us the faithful love God has for His people even in their wandering and unfaithfulness.

THE LAST YEARS OF THE KINGDOM OF JUDAH

Several prophets preached in Judah before and during its destruction: Isaiah, Micah, Nahum, Jeremiah, Habakkuk, and Zephaniah. Isaiah and Micah overlapped our division of times. They lived and preached in Judah both during the Divided Kingdom—the same time as Hosea and Amos—and after the Northern Kingdom was destroyed. See how this all fits together?

* *Of these, which two are called Major Prophets? (You can peek at the previous paragraphs. I totally already gave you the answer.)* _____ *and*

_____.

I think it's so important to at least have a feel for who these fellas were because it changes the way you read their stories. Familiar passages all of a sudden take on new life because you have a sense of the heart behind their messages. For example, find Isaiah 53 and read through it while remembering what you know of Jesus.

Isaiah, a prophet to the nation of Judah who lived hundreds of years before the Christ would come, was telling the people that a Savior would redeem them.

* *List anything from Isaiah 53 that you recognize as descriptive of Christ.*

The other major prophet in Judah during this time period was Jeremiah, who is referred to as "the weeping prophet" because he mourned the downfall of Jerusalem and the destruction of the temple. He had a tough assignment. The false prophets preached good news. They kept saying God was going to rescue the people, but Jeremiah (and we'll see Ezekiel) had to proclaim that

☐ JONAH= preached God's message to the Assyrians

☐ AMOS= urged God's people to turn back to Him

☐ HOSEA= an illustration of God's love for His people

☐ ISAIAH= tells of Jesus hundreds of years before His birth

☐ MICAH= predicted the birth-place of Jesus

☐ ZEPHANIAH= warnings about the Day of the Lord

 DIVIDED KINGDOM

HABAKKUK=
the just shall live
by faith

JEREMIAH=
told God's people they
would be conquered
by the Babylonians

LAMENTATIONS=
mourned the downfall
of Jerusalem
and destruction
of the temple

"No, God isn't going to rescue us. He's sending the Babylonians to conquer and punish us." Ouch.

Based on what you've just learned, read Jeremiah 11:6-11 and see if it makes more sense in light of the context. Are you surprised by a sense of comprehension that you might not have had earlier? I hope so.

The other book listed in the "Major Prophets" section is Lamentations, which isn't the name of a prophet. It's actually written by our weeping buddy Jeremiah after the destruction of Jerusalem as he (you guessed it!) lamented the devastating loss.

We've got more prophets tomorrow, but I think that's enough for today. Well done, friend; we're getting there!

Answers to the opening review: Solomon, foreign, Israel, Judah, Assyrians, Babylonians (I still think it's always the Babylonians), and 70.

Answers to King's portion: 3, 1, 2, 3, 1, 2

 DIVIDED KINGDOM

DAY 5
THE PROPHETS CONTINUED

Believe it or not, this is your last day of homework for the Old Testament. I know it's been hard work, and I imagine there have been times when you felt overwhelmed by information. Despite that, you've stuck with it, and you should be so proud of yourself for your effort.

As we wrap this section up, we're going to finish talking about the other prophets and end things with the foretelling of the coming Savior, Jesus.

   Not all of the prophets spoke to people in Israel and Judah. For example, Obadiah directed his preaching to the people of Edom. They were enemies of Judah and they rejoiced when it fell. Obadiah proclaimed that they would be punished for the way they responded and that eventually the people of Israel would return to their land.

* *Now here's a question that will test your memory: where do we look in Scripture to understand the bad blood between Judah and Edom? Here's a hint: They were the sons of Isaac and Rebekah. Do you remember? If not, go back in your notes and fill in their names.*

_____ *and* _____.

* *Find the Book of Nahum in your Bible and read the first verse. (Again, no shame in using the table of contents, after all, why else did they put it there?) Who was Nahum asked to speak to on behalf of God?*

Nahum preached against Nineveh. I should tell you that Nineveh was the capitol city of Assyria. Yep, same people Jonah preached to about 150 years before. If you're trying to keep score, Jonah preached to Nineveh and they had a revival about 775 B.C., but the revival didn't last because they destroyed the Northern Kingdom about 50 years later. But as they say, what goes around comes around. The Babylonians conquered the Assyrians. Then the Babylonians conquered Judah and took them captive into exile. But then the Persians conquered Babylon and let the Jews come back from exile. Now you know about the Babylonian captivity.

A LIST OF THE CONQUERED

THE ASSYRIANS
→ ISRAEL

THE BABYLONIANS
→ ASSYRIA

THEN

THE BABYLONIANS
→ JUDAH

BUT BE OF GOOD CHEER. BECAUSE THE PERSIANS
→ THE BABYLONIANS

THEN THE PERSIANS
← LET THE JEWS GO HOME

☐ OBADIAH=
preached to Edom

EXILE

☐ NAHUM=
preached to Ninevah

Jeremiah the prophet preached in the time just before and during the first years of the Babylonian captivity. What very specific and distinct thing did Jeremiah prophesy about the captivity? (Jeremiah 25:11-12; 29:10)

The captivity or exile lasted 70 years. While the Jews were there, two prophets spoke to them. They're both "Major Prophets." The first one is Ezekiel. The false prophets of the day kept saying God was going to bless His people. Good times, they were a comin'. Ezekiel preached from Babylon and his message was just the opposite. Instead of good times, Ezekiel preached the judgment of God followed by forgiveness when the people repented. (Both Ezekiel's and Jeremiah's message).

How did Ezekiel act out judgment coming on Jerusalem in Ezekiel 5:1-4?

EZEKIEL WAS THE WILD PROPHET WHO ACTED OUT MANY OF HIS MESSAGES WITH STRANGE ACTIONS.

Ezekiel seems the most eccentric of the prophets because he acted out many of his messages. He did things like scratch the outline of Jerusalem on an adobe brick and lay siege to it or dig through the wall of his house to show people trying to escape Jerusalem.

Like Ezekiel, Daniel also lived in exile and preached to the captive Jews in Babylon.

What happened to Daniel in Daniel 2:46-49?

☐ EZEKIEL=
preached judgment and then forgiveness when the people repented

In verse 49, he requests that some of his friends be put in powerful positions as well. Write down their names.

Ever heard of them? If so, you're imagining a fiery furnace. They were working high up in the ranks of Babylon when the king demanded that they bow down to a golden statue. They refused, and were thrown in the furnace. The king was obviously impressed when they didn't, you know, burn up.

☐ DANIEL=
remained faithful to God during the Babylonian exile

When you think about Daniel, what words come to mind? Maybe "lions' den"? While Daniel is in power, a new king is crowned. He's a fan of being worshiped, and when Daniel doesn't take the bait, he's tossed into a den of lions. Have no fear … he makes it out alive.

 EXILE

Does it change the way you think about Daniel when you have the context of who he was talking to, where he was living, and why it was important? I hope it does. I love making connections like that. It takes us from an isolated story we might be able to recite to understanding where it happened in the scheme of things.

We're almost done, but we've got a couple more prophets to learn about before we close this part of the study.

Joel. Nobody knows for sure where to put Joel. He preached about a locust plague but there's nothing in his book that tells us exactly when he lived. He recognized the judgment came from God, but I love a promise Joel extended to the people.

* *What hope does the passage in the margin signal to you? Could you use hope like that?*

□ JOEL=
preached during a locust plague

I will restore to you the years that the swarming locust has eaten.
JOEL 2:25

THE POST-EXILIC PROPHETS

God sent prophets to preach to the Jews after they returned to the promised land from captivity. The first two were Haggai and Zechariah, who urged the people to rebuild the temple. If you remember details from earlier, they helped Zerubbabel. When things got tough and work on the building lagged, they reminded the Jews how important it was to complete the temple.

Something I really didn't have a firm grasp on was the sheer amount of Old Testament writing predicting the coming Christ. As Christians, we can sometimes read through the New Testament without realizing that the prophets predicted details about Jesus hundreds and hundreds of years before He came—even down to the details of His death.

* *Remembering that Zechariah is speaking to the returning Jews, read Zechariah 12:10. What strikes you about this verse, knowing what you do about the death of Jesus?*

□ HAGGAI=
urged the rebuilding of the temple

□ ZECHARIAH=
ditto

EZRA AND NEHEMIAH

We talked about the return from the exile. The Jews were in Babylon. The city of Jerusalem had been destroyed. The return came about in three stages. Zerubbabel led the first group back (between 539-529 B.C.).

EXILE

* *They rebuilt:*

EZRA=
restored worship
in the temple

Right, they rebuilt the temple, but the city was still destroyed, the walls were torn down, and the people were a mess. Then Ezra (as in the Book of Ezra) led the second group (about 458 B.C.). Ezra restored worship at the temple. Finally Nehemiah led the third group (445 B.C.). Nehemiah rebuilt the wall around Jerusalem.

NEHEMIAH=
rebuilt the wall of
Jerusalem

* *Here's a question: why are Ezra and Nehemiah's books located where they are in the Old Testament?*

ESTHER=
God uses a woman
to save His people

If you guessed that they're located with the histories (Samuel, Kings and Chronicles) because Ezra and Nehemiah weren't prophets, give yourself a star. If you didn't guess that, no worries. I had to research it myself.

THE LAST PROPHET

The last prophet before the Old Testament ends is Malachi, who explicitly tells God's beloved people that they will one day be rescued.

Take just a moment and think about this. Don't gloss over it or let the Enemy of your soul steal the power of this last section. The Jews have been back in their land for about 100 years now. They've gone through a period of revival and are now back to their lackadaisical ways with God.

MALACHI=
last prophet of the
Old Testament

Malachi, the last prophet of the age and the writer of the last sentences we will read in the Old Testament, is shouting words of hope and promise to the people: "He is coming back for us."

This is temporary. Our Savior is coming, and He will make all of this right eventually. We can't do it on our own; heaven knows we've tried.

The temple, while not as grand as Solomon's, has been rebuilt.

Through visions, dreams, and words, mighty prophets of God have been declaring the same thing for years, and it's about to go dark on the scene.

Do you hear those words?

He is coming back for us.

All of this sin, this disobedience, this apathy by God's own people—none of it will prevent Him from claiming His bride.

Who could love like this?

* *Read Malachi 3:1.*

Four hundred years before a baby was born in Bethlehem, a prophet cried out to the people with the words "Behold, He is coming…"

All of these words, these tangled messes of the people in the first books of the Bible, they tell us that it's not over. We have a King who won't be thwarted; He keeps His word and loves His people with a ferocity that defies logic.

Wait for Him, they say.

He will be born humbly, with the flesh of a newborn baby, but don't misunderstand; all authority and power will belong to Him, and His life will draw a line through eternity.

There have been kings, yes.

But after the silence of 400 years, we will hear the words that still our restless souls: the only true King has finally come.

FUN FACT

A TALE OF TWO CITIES

The Babylonians destroyed two cities at about the same time: Nineveh (612 B.C.) and Jerusalem (586 B.C.). Nineveh was the capital of the Assyrian Empire. Jerusalem the capital of Judah. But there the similarities end. As the prophets Nahum and Zephaniah predicted, Nineveh (the site of modern day Mosul, Iraq) disappeared from history and was only rediscovered by archaeologists about 150 years ago. What was the difference? God led Zerubbabel, Ezra, and Nehemiah to rebuild Jerusalem.

Why is that so important? Because the seamless story would have come to an end. No Jerusalem meant no Israel. No Israel, no Messiah. God called Abraham to create a people—Israel—who provided a place and a context for God to send His Son Jesus. Glance at the course map once again and see how God was working all the time … just because He loves you and me.

five

WEEK 5

THE MESSIAH

We're here! We're here! All of what we've done so far—every single word recorded in the Old Testament—has led us to this moment. The Hero of the story is coming to us clothed in flesh and swaddled in blankets.

Yes—Him. The Messiah King. The Suffering Servant. The Redeemer. Jesus, the Christ.

While last week might have had a lot of "wait … who is that?" moments, this one holds the answer. Every person we have met and every story we have read has simply been an arrow pointing to the Lord Jesus.

Before you begin this week, I want you to do something. Forget the fact that you "know the story," and let it wash over you anew in light of the weeks you have completed. Ask the Holy Spirit to bring the Scripture to life as you read about the life and death of Christ.

Our icons are pretty self-explanatory this week, but let's go over them really quickly before we move on. The manger reminds us of the humble beginnings of the Lord. The fish symbol (you've seen that on cars, right?) is our cue to remember the disciples of Christ. Why the fish? Well, that's a good question. And one you'll be able to answer very shortly.

The lamb symbolizes the ministry of Jesus, and the cross … well you probably know what that one means.

I pray that by the end of this week, that cross holds new meaning for you as some of the loose ends we picked up in the Old Testament are woven into the spectacular tapestry of grace that the cross reflects.

And last, but not least, the church. When we get to the end of this week, we will see the beginning of the church forming and we'll understand a bit more about what we are called to be as Jesus' disciples.

This week is all about Him.

Before we even start, bow your head and your heart to Him in praise. Oh, mighty King Jesus we don't understand the way You love us, but we bask in the glow of mercy. Thank You. It's all for You and because of You.

Speak to your servants, Lord.

BORN   DISCIPLES   MINISTRY   DEATH   CHURCH

SESSION 5 THE KINGDOMS AND THE PROPHETS

REVIEW WEEK 4 HOMEWORK

* Review the icons on the course map you've covered so far.

* What was the huge shift in the kingdom that you learned about this week in your homework?

* What or whom have you elevated to the position of king in your life?

* How does true repentance look different from an "I'm sorry?"

* Day 1: Like Saul, do you ever let other people's opinions shape your actions? How does that work out for you?

  • To what conclusion did Samuel immediately jump when he saw Jesse's eldest son? What does God's response (that He looks at the heart, not the outside) mean to you?

* Day 2: Has there been a time when you felt punished by God? How has that affected your relationship with Him?

* Day 3: Solomon began so well and then many wives led his heart away from the Lord. What sorts of things do we deal with that try to lead our hearts away?

* Day 4: What did you see in Isaiah 53 that points you to Jesus?

#seamlessbiblestudy

* Day 5: How does the fact that God predicted the 70 years of the Babylonian captivity encourage or discourage you? Possible thoughts could include:

a. Wow, God was pretty harsh. Seventy years?

b. God was incredibly patient before He sent them into captivity.

c. I bet they thought God had forgotten them.

d. Incredible how God had a plan in mind all the time.

e. All the pieces fit together for our good, but it sure can be painful.

* What hope do you see in Joel 2:25? How could that hope encourage you in your situation?

* The Old Testament ends on a note of hopeful failure. How does the failure of Israel to find the perfect life point to the Messiah God would send?

WATCH SESSION 5: THE KINGDOMS AND THE PROPHETS (VIDEO RUN TIME 12:17)

DAY 1
THE GOSPELS OF MATTHEW & LUKE

Well, you made it. As we start our fifth week together, we are entering a sacred time in history. I hope this week blesses you in a new way because you have a better understanding of how God prepared a context for His Son to arrive.

God's chosen people have been waiting for the promised Messiah to come, and 400 years have passed since the time of the prophet Malachi.
   In those 400 years, the Greeks conquered the promised land. The Jews temporarily took over again, and then the Romans conquered the entire Mediterranean world. As the New Testament begins, Caesar Augustus rules the Roman Empire, and he has appointed several officials to rule over different parts of Israel.

* *Look at the map below and familiarize yourself with the following places: Galilee, Capernaum, Cana, Nazareth, Bethany, Jerusalem, Bethlehem, and Judea.*

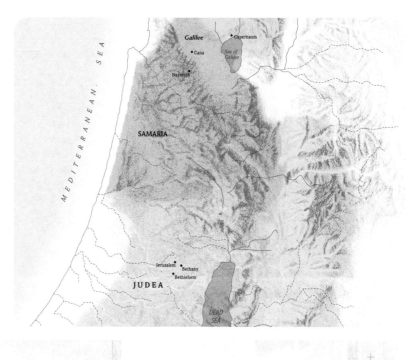

BIRTH

Many prophets had described what the Messiah would be like, where and to whom He would be born, where He would travel, and other details about Him. In every history book you will find evidence that Caesar Augustus was a real person, along with King Herod and many others from this time period. The story isn't a fairy tale; it's documented fact.

The New Testament opens with four books called the Gospels: Matthew, Mark, Luke, and John. They give four accounts of the life of Christ given by different men. Each was written to a specific audience and with a slightly different purpose. The first three are called the synoptic Gospels because of how similar they are. The Book of John takes a little bit of a different approach, and we'll get to that one soon.

Synoptic means *with the same or a common view.* They tell of Jesus from a common viewpoint.

I think the best way to understand the Gospels is to study the life of Christ chronologically, stopping where one differs from another in detail. Sound good? Perfect.

* *Before we jump headfirst into Matthew, skim through the first 17 verses. What is Matthew describing?*

* *Names, names, names. A whole lot of names. Why do you think Matthew gives us all these names?*

☐ MATTHEW=
    the Gospel directed
    to the Jewish people

Matthew was a Jewish follower of Christ who was writing to his fellow Jews. He was appealing to God's chosen people a few decades after Jesus died. He wrote to convince them that Christ was the Messiah for whom they had been waiting.

In Jewish culture, ancestry is critically important, so Matthew starts out with a list tracing Jesus all the way back to Adam.

Oh, wait. No he didn't. He went somewhere else instead.

* *With what two names does he kick things off? (v. 1)*

* *Why do you think he did that? Look up the following verses to help with your answer: Genesis 12:1-3; 2 Samuel 7:8-13.*

BIRTH

Matthew reminds Jewish readers of the two main covenants God made with His people: He told David a King would sit on his throne forever, and He told Abraham that all the families of the earth would be blessed through him. Matthew starts out with a bang, knowing that these names will perk their ears up for the rest.

Over and over throughout his book, Matthew emphasizes that Jesus is the King, and that He came to fulfill what the prophets had predicted about the Messiah. Along those lines, Matthew tells his fellow Jews the way that Christ came into the world.

By all accounts, Mary was young, probably around 15 or 16. This wasn't unusually young to have a baby during this time period, but certainly the way the events unfolded were, um, unprecedented.

* *Read Matthew 1:18-21 and fill in the following:*

When Mary was betrothed (engaged) to _____, she was found to be with child from the _____. And an angel of the Lord appeared to him (Joseph) and told him to take Mary as his _____ and name her son _____ for he will _____.

* *Verse 22 says, "All this took place to _____ what the Lord had spoken by the prophet."*

Well, that sounds interesting. Then Matthew drops in his important fulfillment talk, because he wants his audience to have the promises from the Old Testament soaking their knowledge of Christ. He goes on to quote the prophet Isaiah, who had told the people that exactly this would happen.

* *What do Isaiah 7:14, 9:2-7 predict?*

Hundreds of years before, God whispered prophesies to His representatives on earth. Now Matthew declares to His people that this baby was the awaited Messiah. Matthew continues on his purposeful telling of the birth of Christ, knowing by the Old Testament prophesies that the Messiah would be born in Bethlehem (see Matthew 2:5 and Micah 5:2). But how? Joseph and Mary didn't live there—they lived in Nazareth.

This part of the story happens in the Book of Luke.

 BIRTH

* Read Luke 2:1-7 and in the margin describe what
happened leading Jesus to be born in Bethlehem.

Matthew picks up the story after Jesus was born. Wise men (also called
magi) came from the east following a star. The Book of Matthew is the
only Gospel that records this story.

* Read Matthew 2:1-2 and see if you can figure out
why he included the story in his Gospel to the Jews. Does
anything about his description of Christ line up with his
main objective in presenting his case?

You got it. The wise men were looking for the King. And as we now
know, that is Matthew's favorite Messianic buzzword.
    King Herod (the ruler of Judea) is annoyed about all of this, and
worries that Christ might threaten his throne, so he makes some of
his people look up the records about where the Messiah will be born.
Sure enough, they tell him the place is Bethlehem, and he decides he
better put an end to this madness.

* What does Herod do? (Matthew 2:16)

In a dream God told Joseph this was going to happen, so they fled
to Egypt where they would remain until the wicked Herod was dead.
    And here we go. You ready for this?
    Seriously. It's so good.

* What prophecy do you find in Hosea 11:1?

Are you getting all of this? Using the Old Testament prophets
Matthew is point-by-point laying out his case to show the Jews that
Jesus fulfilled all of their prophecies.
    A virgin and her fiancé have to travel to Bethlehem for a census,
where they deliver a child. In order to escape death, they flee to Egypt,
returning to Israel after the death of the ruler. It's not like this stuff just
happens every day.
    We don't hear much about Jesus' childhood, with the exception
of one particular incident recorded in the Book of Luke.

 BIRTH

□LUKE=
a Gospel known for its
attention to detail

Before we read about that, let's take a second to meet Luke.

The writer of the third Gospel (we'll come back to Mark) is a doctor who loves long walks on the beach and playing Yahtzee by candlelight.

Well, some of that is true.

He was a doctor.

Remember how Matthew was a Jewish believer who preached about Jesus to the Jews? Dr. Luke is coming from a different perspective altogether. In fact, he's the only Gospel writer who is a Gentile.

Also, he is Greek. And we know that he was well educated and a class-A observer, which I sure do appreciate. He cares about the details and it shows in his writing.

While Matthew portrayed Christ as King, Luke shows Him as Man.

* *Just for kicks, look at Luke 3:23-38. To whom does Luke trace Jesus' lineage?*

Exactly. Matthew wanted to show Jesus as the Jewish Messiah. Gentile Luke wanted to show Jesus' connection to Gentiles (a Gentile is anybody who isn't a Jew). If you're emphasizing that Jesus was for all of us, what better place to start than with the father of the whole human race?

OK, before we close for the day let's read Luke's account of Jesus the boy.

* *Read Luke 2:39-52 and describe the gist of what happened.*

* *Jesus tells His parents they should have known He was in the temple, and He calls it, _____ _____ _____.*

Well, well, well. Looks like Someone is hinting at His destiny here.

His ministry hasn't officially started, and it won't for several more years. In fact, Jesus will be 30 years old when we hear from Him again, and we'll meet Him in the water, once again fulfilling prophecies left and right.

 BIRTH

DAY 2
THE GOSPEL OF MARK
& JOHN THE BAPTIST

Mark wrote the second Gospel. His goal was to tell the Romans about Jesus. Mark is the shortest Gospel and is certainly the most practical. He portrays Jesus as a Servant, and spends a lot of time focusing on the deeds of Christ.

Mark displays a very matter-of-fact tone. He doesn't spend time telling about genealogy or prophecy. The Romans were strictly action oriented. So Mark told about Jesus as: "Here's the Guy and this is what He did." That's what his audience cared about—just show me the evidence and don't waste my time.

I'll be honest with you at the risk of you calling me ugly names and slamming this shut. Mark's just not my favorite writer of the bunch. It's probably because I like the narrative, the details, the build-up that comes along with, say, Dr. Detail (Luke). Don't feel bad, Mark. Your class-mates probably voted you "most likely to be efficient" and plenty of folks think you're swell.

That's your crash course in Mark. Now let's move along to the next time we hear updates about Jesus so we can continue to plot the dots of His life on earth.

JOHN THE BAPTIST

* *Read Isaiah 40:3, and then read Matthew 3:1-6. Who is the man doing the baptizing? _____*
(Tired? Don't even worry about looking. I told you the answer in the subheading because I'm a giver.)

Elizabeth was Mary's cousin (Luke 1:36). Your Bible may say that Mary and Elizabeth were "relatives," but the original Greek word used is "cousin," which makes John and Jesus cousins as well.

They may have seen each other in passing (or maybe not—we can speculate but we really don't know) while growing up, but one thing is certain: they haven't grown up together. We can surmise this from the text, as John looks up and sees Christ walking toward him.

FUN FACT:
A Harmony of the Gospels isn't about singing. Bible scholars have compared the four Gospel stories and created books showing every word, side by side, with the events in order. They are really helpful if you want to study all four Gospels.

☐ MARK=
   the action-packed Gospel

DISCIPLES

* *What does he say to Jesus when Jesus asks to be baptized? (Matthew 3:14)*

John's job was to prepare the way for the Messiah, and in the verses previous to this one, we hear him clearly telling the people that he isn't the One they're waiting for. Read Matthew 3:11-12 and fill in the following:

MATTHEW 10:2-4 LISTS THE 12 DISCIPLES JESUS CALLED:

1. Simon (Peter)
2. Andrew
3. James, son of Zebedee
4. John
5. Philip
6. Bartholomew
7. Thomas
8. Matthew
9. James, son of Alphaeus
10. Thaddaeus
11. Simon, the Zealot
12. Judas Iscariot

* *"I baptize you with _____ for repentance, but he who is coming after me is mightier than I, whose sandals I am not worthy to carry. He will _____ you with the _____ _____ and _____."*

John had no question in his mind when he looked upon Christ—he knew Jesus was the promised King. After Christ is baptized, the Spirit leads Him into the wilderness for 40 days where Satan tests Him. Over and over, He rebukes the Enemy by using Scripture, and at the end of that time He returns to Galilee and officially begins His ministry on earth.

He isn't going to do it alone though, and Jesus starts calling men to follow Him. Specifically, He invites 12 men along for the journey.

Jesus is a charismatic, likeable Teacher, and He fascinates people everywhere He goes. In one of His most often-quoted speeches, He lays out the laws of His kingdom. The Sermon on the Mount (Matthew 5–7) is a beautiful description of what we are called to be as Christians. It covers topics such as caring for the poor, being the salt and light to our world, loving our enemies, knowing how to pray, and the Golden Rule—treat others the way you would want them to treat you (Matthew 7:12).

Proving He is the Son of God, Jesus goes on to perform many miracles including the healing of leprosy, calming a storm, healing a paralytic, healing blindness, and exorcising demons.

* *In Matthew 10:1, Jesus gives the 12 apostles a unique authority. What is it?*

* *He sends them out to tell people that the kingdom of God is at hand, but the message is only sent to one group at this point. Who is it? (Matthew 10:5-6)*

 DISCIPLES

* *Why do you think Matthew makes a point of mentioning this?*

The lost sheep of Israel. They are God's chosen people and He wants them to return to Him.

Jesus warns the apostles that following Him will not be easy, and His words echo through our lives even to this day as believers:

> *"You will be hated by all for my name's sake."*
> **MATTHEW 10:22**

Interesting recruiting strategy, eh? "People will hate you. Sign up here."

* *When have you felt hated or disliked because of your beliefs? How did you react?*

Jesus knew that many people wouldn't accept Him as the Messiah and He even knew that two of His own apostles would fail Him. And yet, He loved them, served them, and ministered to them in spite of it. His heart was always engaged, and I imagine His eyes lit up when He talked about the will of His Father.

Even those who refused to believe Jesus was God were drawn to His teaching and crowds gathered around Him wherever He went. Often He would teach using parables, which were simply stories that used analogies to present truth.

* *See Matthew 13:18-23 for Jesus' explanation of a parable. What message did Jesus convey through the story?*

Jesus continues traveling with His apostles and performing miracles until one day when He breaks the shocking news to them.

* *In Matthew 16:21 what did Jesus begin to tell them was going to happen?*

DISCIPLES

They don't want to believe it! Their Christ? Their Friend? No. It can't be.

But it is, and in a matter of time Jesus will return to Jerusalem, to the Mount of Olives, where He will ride into the city on a donkey's back while the people shout,

> "Hosanna to the Son of David! Blessed is
> he who comes in the name of the Lord!"
> **MATTHEW 21:9**

But not even this moment happened by chance; not even the smallest detail was left to the imagination.

* *Read Zechariah 9:9 and record the prediction made about the coming Messiah.*

If you were a Jew who knew the Old Testament, wouldn't you have been staring at this man, piecing together all of the details, and committing your life to Him? You would think so, but such wasn't the case for many.

A significant amount of rumbling about Jesus goes on among the people, and the religious leaders are getting sick of hearing about Him. They're threatened by Him and hungry for power, so they set the wheels in motion for the saddest day in history—a day when the ground would shake and the heavens would cry out in agony.

Behold, the Messiah has come, and the Light of the world will soon be extinguished by the disbelief of men and women.

 DISCIPLES

DAY 3
GETHSEMANE

The more attention Christ got, the more enemies He made. The Pharisees were slaves to the law who refused to see past what they felt was rule-breaking on His behalf. Jesus healed people on the Sabbath day, which was considered a day where work was prohibited. He criticized them for being blind to what He was doing, but they wouldn't budge.

The Pharisees were so "law, law, law" that they couldn't see past it. But the Pharisees weren't the only group who resented Jesus; the Scribes and Sadducees were also angered by His words and actions. Jesus was a threat to all three groups for slightly different reasons. Eventually, they decided that something had to be done to remove the threat.

* *Jesus told His disciples what was coming. What did Jesus say was going to happen? (Matthew 26:1-5) Who gathered together to plot Jesus' arrest?*

* *What was the reasoning in waiting until after the Passover to arrest Him?*

The religious leaders were afraid of what men might do. They didn't want an uproar. They didn't want a spectacle to distract them from keeping their customs and traditions. Mostly they didn't want anything to threaten their position of authority—even if it was the very God they were supposedly serving.

Do you see how ridiculously ironic this is? They are so busy pointing to every jot and tittle in the books that they miss the Man who came to save their souls. God forbid we should do the same.

THREE GROUPS MADE UP THE LEADERSHIP OF THE JEWISH COMMUNITY IN JESUS' DAY.

1. The Sadducees were Hellenized Jews (they had adopted Greek culture and thought). They did not believe in a resurrection. We might identify them as the liberals of the day. Their power base was the temple and Jerusalem.
2. The Scribes were the lawyers. They were the authorities on the Jewish law.
3. The Pharisees were the Jewish conservatives. They sought to follow the Jewish law and shun Greek thought. Their power base was outside the city of Jerusalem. The Pharisees and Sadducees were natural enemies.

MINISTRY

* *How do we today face the same dilemma? How do we sometimes have to choose between obedience to God and concern for what people will think of us?*

Among the disciples was a man named Judas Iscariot, who would betray Christ for 30 pieces of silver.

* *If you're looking for examples of prophesy, what happened to the 30 pieces of silver? (Zechariah 11:12-13)*

After betraying Jesus, Judas changed his mind and tried to return the money. They refused and Judas hung himself in shame.

* *Read Matthew 27:3-10 and describe what happened in verse 7 to the 30 pieces of silver Judas had received as a reward.*

The night before this betrayal happened, Jesus gathered His disciples for the Passover meal where He predicted the betrayal and instituted something we still celebrate in our churches today.

Jesus broke bread and explained that it was to be considered His body, eaten in remembrance of what He would do on the cross. Likewise, He used the wine to show His blood, which would be poured out for the forgiveness of our sins.

As they leave the upper room, the disciples follow Jesus as they have for many months, this time to the Mount of Olives where Christ will tell them that Judas isn't the only disciple who will betray Him.

* *Who else does Jesus say will deny Him? How many times? (Matthew 26:30-35)*

There, in the darkness of night and the thick of the garden, the Savior of the world cries out in sorrow. He begs His disciples to stay awake with Him, but they fall asleep, leaving Him alone with His Father God—and with the burden of choosing to die for us.

 MINISTRY

✳ *In Matthew 26:39 and 42, what does Jesus ask of His Father?*

The cup represents the entire ordeal of suffering and dying on behalf of a rebellious world. The cup isn't going to pass.

The hour has come for Judas Iscariot to arrive with a great crowd of people armed with weapons and anger. With a kiss, Judas identifies Christ, and the soldiers take Jesus away to Caiaphas, the high priest.

Plenty of people ponied up with stories intended to condemn Jesus, but in the end they were all false witnesses and none could provide what the jury of priests needed to condemn Him according to the law.

In the face of these accusations, Jesus remained silent. Read Isaiah 53:7 if you're looking for a little prophecy about this.

Jesus' refusal to address the charges just infuriated the priests, and finally they pressed Him with these words:

> *"Tell us if you are the Christ, the Son of God."*
> **MATTHEW 26:63**

It's a direct question, and the answer Jesus gives—"You have said so ..." (Matthew 26:64)—is enough to accuse Him of blasphemy. He is sentenced to death on a cross— an execution reserved for the lowest of the low.

While Jesus is being held, in accordance with Christ's prophesy, Peter denies Jesus three times. Don't forget that this happened, because when we meet up with Peter again, we'll see a much different side of him. A side that reminds us we are all unworthy, and yet, loved beyond measure.

In the morning, they bring Jesus to Pilate, the governor. As you remember, the Romans rule Israel at this time. Now, let's back up the truck for one second.

✳ *Of what was Jesus being accused? (Matthew 26:65)*

✳ *According to Leviticus 24:16, what is the punishment for this crime?*

The leaders wanted Jesus killed, but they wanted someone else to blame. So they brought Him to the Roman governor. They knew Pilate would care nothing for punishing the religious crime of blasphemy, so

MINISTRY

they changed the charges. They ramped up the political angle to force Pilate to become involved.

* *Of what did the Jewish leaders accuse Jesus before Pilate? (Luke 23:1-2)*

In other words, "Hey, Pilate? He's not honoring Rome, nor is He encouraging us to honor Rome. You better step in before there's a power struggle. We're just looking out for you, you know …"

Pilate tries to avoid murdering Jesus, and appeals to Herod in Galilee to do it instead once he hears that Jesus belonged to his jurisdiction. Herod doesn't find Jesus guilty and sends Him back to Pilate.

Now Pilate is between a rock and a hard place. He knows the Jews will be furious if Jesus lives, but he has the hunch that He isn't actually guilty. Not to mention, his wife had a dream warning him not to be a part of the death of Christ.

Every Passover, it was customary to release one person from jail, so Pilate comes up with a plan. He'll tell them that it's either Christ or the notorious and dangerous murderer, Barabbas. He'll release their choice. Surely they'll pick Christ, right?

Wrong.

In the face of choosing between a dangerous murderer and the man who claims to be God's Son, they opt to let the murderer loose on their streets.

Would we do the same?

I shudder to think we would, but the reality is clear: our nature refuses to acknowledge God's sovereignty, and we would put ourselves in harm's way before confessing He is the One.

And Jesus, our Savior, the promised King of the world, will be put to death on our behalf.

The Lamb, led to slaughter, will become our righteousness.

Have mercy on us, Lord. We choose everything before You and You refuse to do the same in return.

 MINISTRY

DAY 4
THE CRUCIFIXION & RESURRECTION

Shouts echoed throughout Jerusalem, "Free Barabbas! Free Barabbas!" and Pilate shook his head, shocked at their envy and hatred.

* *We see one of the most chilling examples of the power of influence in Luke 23:23. What does the second half of the verse say?*

And that was it.

Jesus would be hung on a cross, exactly as they wanted. It was no surprise to Him; He had referenced the way He would die well before the unlikely method was chosen.

* *What does Jesus tell His disciples about His death in Matthew 20:17-19?*

Knowing that Jesus was being falsely accused, Pilate tries to satisfy the accusers by having Jesus beaten. The soldiers twist a crown of thorns, pressing it deep into the flesh of Jesus. They mock the Savior, strip Him naked, spit on Him, and beat Him until He is limp and damp with blood. You can read about it in Luke 23:16 and John 19:1-5.

Finally, against his better judgment, Pilate delivers Christ to his soldiers to be murdered. They parade Jesus throughout the streets of Jerusalem and nail Him to a cross. To mock Jesus for His claims, above the cross of Christ they hang a sign with the words, "King of the Jews." The guards split Christ's clothing four ways, but when they came to His tunic, they cast lots to see who would get it.

CROSS

JOHN 19:23-24

When the soldiers had crucified Jesus, they took his garments and divided them into four parts, one part for each soldier; also his tunic. But the tunic was seamless, woven in one piece from top to bottom, so they said to one another, "Let us not tear it, but cast lots for it to see whose it shall be." This was to fulfill the Scripture which says, "They divided my garments among them, and for my clothing they cast lots." So the soldiers did these things.

PSALM 22:18

They divide my garments among them, and for my clothing they cast lots.

*   Compare John 19:23-24 and Psalm 22:18 (printed in the margin). What was unique about the tunic as opposed to other garments of clothing?

*   What prophesy did this fulfill?

A slow, tormenting death on a cross was reserved for murderers, thieves, and the like. Crucifixion was the most shameful, vile way to die and was unparalleled for brutality and humiliation.

In the garden of Eden, God poured out His love by creating humankind.

In the garden of Gethsemane, Jesus the Christ sweat drops of blood in agony as He anticipated His crucifixion.

Up a hill called Golgotha our Lord's feet stumbled as He carried His own cross. While they tortured and ridiculed Him, nailing His hands and feet to the cross, Jesus remained silent—except to ask for God's mercy, not on Himself but on those who drove the nails.

> "Father, forgive them, for they
>   know not what they do."
>   **LUKE 23:34**

For hours, He hung; the weight of all the sin of the world balanced between the narrow beams of wood.

This isn't fiction, and it isn't a dramatization.

Not only was Jesus the King of the Jews, He was the King of all kings. Rejected by the sheep of Israel, the Messiah stretched out His arms in submission to His Father God, unwilling that any of them should perish in their sin.

*   What happened in the moment Jesus died? (Matthew 27:51)

And here's where it comes together—this story we've traced from Genesis. The curtain was torn. Gone. Eliminated. Unnecessary.

No longer does separation divide a Holy God from us because the Christ has come to bring us near. Jesus became the ultimate Lamb, sacrificed on Passover, covering us with the blood of reconciliation forever.

How could it be, you ask?

Why would He rescue us?

I don't know completely, but I do know this: He did, and as a result, you and I stand in the shadow of redemption.

Christ's lifeless body was wrapped in a linen shroud and placed in a tomb cut from stone. To close off the tomb, a large stone was placed at the entrance.

As tradition dictated, the women would treat Christ's body with a blend of different spices after His death. Taking the spices they prepared, several of the women who had known Jesus went to His tomb after the Sabbath, wondering how they were going to move the heavy stone to get to the body of their beloved friend.

When they got there, the stone was pushed aside, the entrance wide open for vandalism. With so much hatred aimed toward Christ, it was easy to imagine someone would have come and taken His remains. But their panic was short-lived, as an angel spoke from inside the tomb.

* *What does the angel say? (Matthew 28:5-6)*

They stared, mystified. All that remained of Christ's burial was His linen cloth, folded where He once lay. They stumbled back to the disciples, shouting the good news, but it was hard to believe; after all, He was dead and buried.

I think about what the disciples must have felt when they heard the news. I imagine they were elated, overwhelmed, and desperate to see Him with their own eyes. But I also wonder if they were hesitant to trust that it was true. They had seen Jesus bring people back to life. They had seen the seas calm in response to His voice. They had witnessed health where sickness had reigned and prayer that commanded peace.

I wasn't there, so I didn't see it firsthand, but I have seen what I would call miracles in my own life. I've felt His presence, His power, and His tenderness toward me in undeniable ways. I suppose you could say I have been to the tomb, and I've stretched my neck to get a glimpse of His deity, only to find the evidence He has left behind.

* *What about you? How have you seen evidence of Jesus in the world? in the lives of those around you? in your own life?*

CROSS

I haven't seen Him face to face, and I haven't touched the hem of His robe. I have heard the voice of Mary the Magdalene in my mind, "He healed me from demons—only God could do that. And now … well, now … the tomb is empty. He was, is, and will always be the Christ."

But my ears and my eyes and my heart are clothed in humanity, and as much as I long to rest in the proof, I wrestle with it instead.

* *In what ways do you wrestle with believing in Jesus? in His promises? in His character?*

* *Why do you think that is?*

Even with what they knew of Jesus, His disciples struggled to believe He had been raised from the dead.

* *In Mark 16:14, why does Jesus rebuke them?*

I know, I know … we haven't talked about John yet. And that's a shame, because he's pretty amazing. His Gospel is different from the other three and is one of the most beautiful writings in all of Scripture.

Up until now, we've seen three different writers direct their work to three different groups, but John has a different plan: He's writing for everyone. Jew or Gentile, Roman or Greek, he's intent on translating for us the most important word we can associate with a true relationship with Christ: *believe.*

JOHN=
the Gospel urging
everyone to believe

John's Gospel reads differently from the others. His telling of the Jesus story is (again, Mark, this is nothing personal) my favorite. If you care about people believing in Christ as the Son of God, you might just share the story of a guy who struggled in his faith.

I would be hard pressed to tell you I have a favorite story in the Bible, mostly because I have issues with this kind of commitment. I mean,

CHURCH

I might change my mind before you carve the tombstone, so let's just play it cool for now. But still. It's so good.

* *Open your Bible to John 20:19-29 and read the account, summarizing it in your own words.*

Thomas. In truth, he's the disciple I relate to most. He's gotten a bad rap for being a doubter, but he was actually a very loyal follower of Christ. He's packing a punch with his little tirade, but my hunch is that the root of it is not unbelief; rather, it's a desperate desire to believe fully.

And I get it. I don't question God because I want to prove He doesn't exist. I question because I want to rest in unshakable faith.

I won't get to see the evidence Thomas did, but it's worth noting that despite all of his ranting and threatening, Scripture never tells us that Thomas actually touched the risen Christ.

Whatever he saw was enough for him to declare Jesus as his Lord and his God. That gentle reminder weaves its way through all of my days. I believe Jesus says to each of us, "You may not get the evidence you say you need to believe in Me, but rest assured, love, I'll give you enough."

Oh, John. What would we do without you?

CHURCH

DAY 5
THE BEGINNING OF THE CHURCH

Let's start our last day this week together by filling in a chart. What? Charts are fun. And you'll feel super accomplished, which is a great way to end the week.

Name of Gospel	Intended Audience	Main Message of Gospel

Well, look at you. Well done, sister. If this was on your bucket list, you're welcome. I'm all about making dreams come true. Up next? Paris. And then, Disney World.

So this week we've been focused on the life and death of Christ, and we'll wrap it up by talking about His final words and the way His disciples carried them forth. Jesus appeared alive on the earth for 40 days after His resurrection, and at that point, His Father took Him up to heaven (called the "ascension").

Before He ascended, He gave a command to those who had followed Him. See Matthew 28:19 and Mark 16:15-16. This is what is called The Great Commission and there's a statement in here that you should definitely pay attention to.

* *Fill in the blanks based on Mark 16:15-16. Wait … Mark cares about getting stuff done? Well, that's entirely shocking (or not at all).*

 CHURCH

"Go into _____ the _____ and proclaim the gospel to the _____ creation. _____ believes and is baptized will be _____ but _____ does not believe will be _____."

Jesus is clear about their mission: tell everyone about Me. Go to the entire world. Every tribe. Every nation. Everyone.

Those who believe will be saved. Not just the Jews, but every single person who believes. You have to understand; this is radical thinking for the time period. R-A-D-I-C-A-L.

The Jews are the ones who observe the law, who are God's special, chosen people. For centuries they've been waiting for their Savior, and looking into the final words of the Messiah sheds light upon God's ultimate plan for humanity. But Christ is also clear about one thing He wants the disciples to do before they run out and start telling everyone the good news.

* *What did Jesus command in Luke 24:49?*

Jerusalem isn't exactly the safest place for them to hang out, but they do so because Christ told them that they had to wait. Ten days after His ascension, on the day of Pentecost, an amazing thing happened.

* *What was it? (Acts 2:1-4)*

In John 14:15-17, Jesus promised His followers a "Helper" who would dwell with us and be within us: the Holy Spirit. Immediately following the welcoming of the Holy Spirit, Peter delivers a sermon to everyone present, and he is not mincing words.

Peter's audience believes he is telling the truth, and from their lips we hear one of the most important questions ever posed in Scripture.

* *What did they ask, and what did the apostles tell them? (Acts 2:37-39)*

PENTECOST IS THE JEWISH FESTIVAL 50 DAYS AFTER PASSOVER TO CELEBRATE A HARVEST (BARLEY). FOR THE CHURCH IT MARKS THE WORLDWIDE HARVEST OF THOSE WHO COME TO CHRIST. WE ARE THE HARVEST.

CHURCH

□ ACTS=
the beginning
of the church

To the Jews listening, this was really controversial; after all, keeping the Law of Moses was the ultimate test of spirituality. What was the purpose of having all of those laws if it wasn't to guarantee your position with God?

Well, that's exactly the point.

Nobody, nowhere, in any way, shape, or form, has ever (EVER) been able to live a perfect life. Until Jesus. He did what we could never do, and His spotless life and brutal death replaced the law as our standard. No more need for blood sacrifices; He did it on our behalf. Perfectly.

When the temple curtain tore, we gained access to God through Jesus, who bore our sins to free us from the penalty—eternal suffering.

The Book of Acts says that those listening were cut to the heart, asking Peter what needed to be done in order to be a follower of Christ. And what does he say?

Repent.

Acknowledge that you deserved the punishment that He took and be baptized as a symbol of your faith, so that you will bear witness to others. Remember how circumcision was a symbol of faith in the Old Testament? Well, now it's baptism.

After the Holy Spirit came, the ministry of Christ began to travel through the world in the order He predicted it would. As you can imagine, it caused quite a stir. People weren't always welcoming of the message, and the church was persecuted as a result. As we see the first man martyred for his faith, we also meet a man who will shape the rest of the New Testament. In the way that He always does, God picks the least likely candidate to change the world.

✳ Read Acts 7:54–8:3. Who died and who was the man who approved his death and proceeded to ravage the church?

Saul was a devout Jew who had been trained by one of the most highly respected rabbis around. He, like many others, saw Christianity as a threat to his faith and the role of the Law of Moses.

Are you ready for this guy? Oh my word. It's *so good*.

Saul has an encounter that will radically alter his life.

 CHURCH

* *Read Acts 9:1-22 and record the bones of the story.*

The hater. The persecutor. The disbeliever. He will become the man to write nearly half of the books of the New Testament.

I just can't even begin to tell you what that means to me.

But wait? Saul? What, you don't remember all that many books of the Bible being written by a fella named Saul? You're right. And many people believe that God changed Saul's name to Paul after his conversion, but that's not actually what happened. In fact, God didn't change his name at all. Let me explain.

Saul was the Hebrew name given to him at his birth. Paul is the Roman version of the same name (his father was a Roman citizen, thus he inherited citizenship), and as someone who was chosen to preach the good news to the Gentiles (or non-Jews), he began going by the name they would be the most familiar with.

The rest of the Book of Acts follows the expansion of the gospel to many different lands by a few key people. We'll keep hearing from Peter and Paul, and we'll be introduced to Timothy, Barnabas, and Silas as we go. They're all missionaries God calls to different places to proclaim His truth. We'll even meet a fellow named James, the half brother of Jesus.

Paul is the main character of Acts. As we read the rest of the book (which I recommend doing when you can make time—it's a really good read!) we follow his journeys and eventually his imprisonment and trial. In our last session together, we're going to study his life in a little more detail, but I wanted to introduce you before we left the Book of Acts.

Now, when I tell you that the Book of Romans was just a letter Paul wrote to the people of Rome, you'll know the context to make sense of it. See? It's all coming together.

I can't wait to finish this up with you! Stick with it—you're SO CLOSE!

CHURCH

WEEK 6
THE LETTERS

We need to understand the chapters that follow the life and death of Jesus, because they bring to light the struggles and stories of fellow believers with their newfound faith. Many times I find myself lost in Paul's words, remembering how his ministry began and what God would call him to be.

You know, Jesus didn't come for the rich, the educated, the popular, or the esteemed folks. He came for me. For us. The beggars and misfits who say we're devoted and then fall asleep as Jesus sweats blood in Gethsemane. His wild grace covers us and rewrites our lives.

We're going to spend time with important people in this last section. I promise you're going to see yourself more than you expected. As Jesus ascends into heaven, His people find themselves in a difficult place, persecuted for their beliefs—hence the handcuff icon. Their stories combine passion and agony that will inspire you no matter what you're facing.

Here we come to a turning point that affects most of us. I'm not Jewish. I'm a Gentile. And that, according to the Old Testament, leaves me outside the bounds of God's highest favor. See those little people icons? They should make you smile. God is about to shift everything to include us, and I guarantee you will understand that differently because of all your hard work these past few weeks.

The gospel of Jesus spread through the letters and words of His followers—see the icons of the map and the letter? These letters comprise a good bit of the words you've either chosen to embroider or put on a chalkboard. It's good, meaty, valuable advice from people who suffered for their faith.

Finally the last book of the Bible—Revelation. That glowing globe symbolizes the new heaven and earth. That's good news for a whole lot of reasons. Right this minute, it's a good reminder for a weepy writer who isn't quite ready for the journey to end. Because it doesn't, friends. Finish this week strong, and when you close this book for the last time, I want you to hear me saying these words to you …

This was just the beginning.

PERSECUTION   GENTILES   SPREAD   LETTERS   REVELATION

SESSION 6 THE MESSIAH

REVIEW WEEK 5 HOMEWORK

* What new things did you grasp from the Scripture this week in your homework?

* Day 1: What clues did we see indicating that Matthew wrote the story of Jesus the Messiah with a focus on Jewish readers? How did Matthew seek to present Jesus?

• What aspect of Jesus' birth and young life as told by Matthew most impressed, surprised, or intrigued you?

* Day 2: Why was John the Baptist reluctant to baptize Jesus?

• What unique authority did Jesus give to the 12 apostles? How do you think believers today relate to the tasks Jesus gave the apostles?

• What did Jesus begin to tell His disciples in passages like Matthew 16:21?

* Day 3: Who gathered together to plot to arrest Jesus? What do you think motivated them?

• How do we sometimes have to choose between obeying God and concern for what people will think of us?

* Day 4: What happened in the moment Jesus died? (Matthew 27:51) What significance do you see in that happening?

• How have you seen evidence of Jesus in the world? in the lives of those around you? in your own life?

* Day 5: What are the four Gospels, the intended audiences, and the goals of each Gospel writer?

• What happened in Acts 9:1-22? What happened as a result?

* Discuss the course map and the meaning of all the icons so far. Do you think you could use the icons to tell a child the story of the Bible?

WATCH SESSION 6: THE LETTERS (VIDEO RUN TIME 11:41)

DISCUSS

* How would you explain the temple veil being torn to a friend? How would you help them grasp the spiritual significance of this moment?

* What new truths did you learn about Jesus this week?

DAY 1
PAUL'S JOURNEYS BEGIN

In the Book of Acts, we learned about Paul and briefly touched on how he traveled around preaching about Christ and urging people (especially Gentiles) to come to faith. We're going to start out this session by looking at the order of his travels, because I think that might be the best way to understand the next several books we are going to study.

But (and I'm sorry about this), I have to warn you. We are going to go in chronological order, and if you recall, that's not necessarily how things show up in the Bible. I know. It's tricky. We find the order from clues in the letters themselves and from the story of the spread of the faith in the Book of Acts.

Paul sets off with his unfortunately-named partner in crime, Barnabas, on the first of three missionary journeys. He would later be joined by some other guys: Mark, Silas, and Timothy.

I'm going to be honest here. The maps of Paul's journeys contain a lot of cities and a lot of details that run together in my mind, and I may never get to a place where I can name every single one in order on all three journeys.

The good news (pun fully intended) is that Jesus still loves me.

So, here's the basic scenario, and then we'll zoom in for more details. I know this is going to look like a lot of information, but bear with me. It helps so much to have the bird's eye view of these things. Note that for things like the order of books or the date they were written you'll find lots of opinions. I adapted these dates from George Guthrie's study called *Read the Bible for Life*.[1] Don't think of them as dates in a history class. Rather think of them as the details you would remember about a good friend. It's part of knowing somebody.

Paul was born in Tarsus of Cilicia, A.D. 10 (Acts 22:3).

Jesus' death and resurrection took place about A.D. 29 or 30, so when Jesus died, Paul was about the age of a typical modern college student. Paul played cheerleader for the murder of Stephen. Then while Paul was seeking to earn his merit badge for persecuting Christians, he encountered the resurrected Jesus sometime between A.D. 34-37.

1. George H. Guthrie, *Read the Bible for Life* (Nashville: LifeWay Press, 2010).

PERSECUTION

* *To see Paul's own description of what happened after he met Jesus, read Galatians 1:15-18. What three places did Paul go and how much time elapsed?*

Some people have compared Paul's three years in Arabia and Damascus to the time many students spend in seminary, but in fact Paul's whole life had been spent learning the Old Testament.

The following chart combines the events of Paul's life with his approximate age for each event or missionary journey and the letters he wrote that became parts of our New Testament.

Paul's Age	Events of Paul's Life
0	Born in Tarsus, A.D. 10 (Acts 22:3)
20	Crucifixion of Jesus A.D. 29–30
24	Stoning of Stephen/Damascus Road (Paul's salvation)
	Silent years A.D. 37–46
36	First Missionary Journey A.D. 46–47
	Galatians(?)
38	Jerusalem Conference A.D. 48–49 (Acts 15)
40	Second Missionary Journey A.D. 50–52
	1 & 2 Thessalonians
43	Third Missionary Journey A.D. 53–57
	1 Corinthians, Galatians(?)
47	Trip to Jerusalem with Offering
	2 Corinthians, Romans
47	Arrest and imprisonment (2 yrs) A.D. 57–59
	Trip to Rome as prisoner
50	First Roman imprisonment A.D. 60–62
	Ephesians, Philippians
	Colossians, Philemon
54	Released from prison A.D. 63–65
	1 Timothy, Titus
57	Final imprisonment and martyrdom A.D. 66–67
	2 Timothy

If you are any kind of Christian, you've memorized the events in that chart and are ready to move on.

 PERSECUTION

Kidding. I'm kidding.

But seriously, I know that looks like a ton of facts and maybe you can't quite sort them out, but I want you to have it in front of you as we look at the rest of the Bible.

Let's go in order. Understanding the Bible chronologically means we jump to 1 and 2 Thessalonians.

You can read about Paul's first missionary journey in Acts 13–14. He probably didn't write any letters during that first trip (some scholars

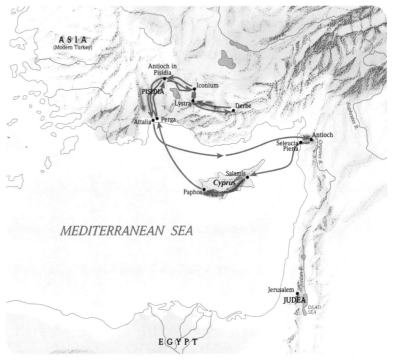

think he wrote Galatians). He was hanging out in the area we know as Turkey (Roman Asia and Galatia) and getting his bearings as a traveling missionary.

On his second missionary journey (described in Acts 15–17), Paul, with Timothy and Silas, stopped in Thessalonica, Greece. After he left, he wrote them a letter to encourage them in their newfound faith. Because he had heard they seemed to be misunderstanding the return of Christ, Paul focused on setting the record straight.

☐ 1 & 2 THESSALONIANS= Paul encouraging the church at Thessalonica

* *Describe at least one promise Paul extended to these young believers 1 Thessalonians 4:13-18.*

 PERSECUTION

See? Doesn't it make a little more sense now? Gracious, I'm praying it does. Paul handwrote the letter and had Timothy deliver it to the new church at Thessalonica a short time after first coming to them.

We can tell that 2 Thessalonians was written shortly after the first letter because Silas and Timothy are still with Paul.

* *What emotions does 2 Thessalonians 2:2 suggest the people in the new church might have been feeling?*

Yeah. They're rattled. They don't understand the second coming of Christ and Paul wants to set their minds at ease. That's the heart of both of these letters.

After his stay in Athens, Paul traveled to Corinth. During Paul's lifetime, the city of Corinth was the commercial center of Greece. He spent a year and a half there establishing a church.

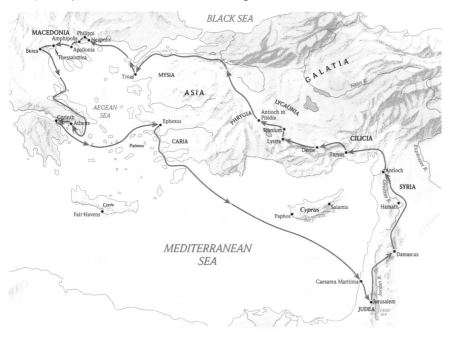

* *Flip over to Acts 18 and read verses 1-11. Who did Paul stay with? _____ and his wife _____.*

PERSECUTION

* Who is Paul testifying to at this point in his ministry?
(Acts 18:5)

* What happens as a result of his frustration with them?
(Acts 18:6)

After starting the church in Corinth, Paul returned to report to his home church in Antioch. He soon sets out on his third trip to Asia and Europe. It lasted for about 4 years and is covered in Acts 18:23–21:16.

On this third missionary journey Paul wrote 1 Corinthians from Ephesus to address some of the many problems in that turbulent congregation. If you ever get discouraged with the imperfections among God's people, just read 1 Corinthians. Talk about a messed up bunch!

Hoping the letter did some good, Paul sent a messenger to see how they were doing. The report came back saying, in essence, "Most everyone in the church gets what you're saying, but some of them aren't sure you're really an apostle. They say they don't know if they should believe you because you weren't one of the 12 that Jesus chose."

So he writes another letter explaining that yes, he is an apostle, and no, he will not be back to visit them because of the pain he has caused.

God bless him, Paul loves a little drama.

GENTILES

He is legitimately making a case for himself, and he's not doing it delicately. Read 2 Corinthians 11:5-11. Tell me you can hear his voice trembling while he defends himself.

But he's about to launch into the meat of his defense.

* *Read 2 Corinthians 11:22-33. List a couple of the things he says about himself. Because my goodness, there are plenty.*

☐ 1 CORINTHIANS=
Paul to the turbulent church in Corinth

☐ 2 CORINTHIANS=
Paul encouraging the church in Corinth to be comforted by Christ

The man is on fire. He is everything you are and a bag of chips. He almost got stoned to death. Had sleep issues. And danger. Lots and lots and lots of danger.

I feel certain that Paul could stand a little PTSD therapy at this point. Ironically, the major point of the second letter to the Corinthian church is that they should be comforted by Christ.

Oh, Paul. We do love you.

Some scholars place the writing of the Book of Galatians between the first and second letters to the Corinthian church. Evidently Paul was short on hobbies.

☐ GALATIANS=
Jesus came to set us free

* *What happened in Galatians 2:11-14? (BTW, Cephas is another name for Peter)*

Remember, Paul is preaching mostly to Gentiles, and Peter's audience is Jewish. We started to talk about this last week, but it's worth revisiting.

Jews have to be circumcised, and all of a sudden the Christians are facing a dilemma. Do Gentiles who believe in Christ have to be circumcised as well? I'm willing to bet that if this went to vote we would see a unanimous response, but fortunately we don't have to do that because Christ gave us the answer and Paul reveals it.

* *Based on Galatians 2:16, what justifies a person?*

GENTILES

It's a new day! The yoke of slavery that came with the law has been released from our necks, and Christ has come to save us and set us free from all of these requirements.

* *Read Galatians 5:2-6. What's the heart of the passage? It's the main message of the Book of Galatians. Write it here:*

The law can't help us; only the Lord can.

And with that, you pat yourself on the back and take a break. Good work today.

 GENTILES

DAY 2
PAUL'S LETTERS TO CHURCHES

The next letter we read from Paul stands as the only one he writes to a church he hasn't actually been to yet. He does want to get to Rome, though.

As someone with my vantage point I feel a little like telling Paul that going to Rome is going to turn out the same way it did for Rose on the Titanic. Leave the blue diamond, Paul. Just kiss it goodbye, because it's not going to be the Hallmark™ moment you've imagined.

☐ ROMANS=
Paul's explanation of Christian beliefs

Sorry. Getting ahead of myself. Anyway, as a Roman citizen Paul obviously feels a calling to Rome even though he hasn't met them and told them about Jesus. So he sends a letter to the church there and he starts off with a some items from his résumé.

* *Fill in the blanks from Romans 1:1-7. "Paul, a* _____ *of Christ Jesus, called to be an _____,* _____ _____ *for the gospel of God."*

Hi. I'm Angie. I've been set apart. It's my go-to introduction at parties and such. I'm just saying, it's bold.

And again, I think Paul is hilarious in his word choices. I get that he wants them to know that he's a devoted follower of Christ and yada yada yada, but please read Romans 1:11 and try to keep a straight face.

Seriously. I hope I can come and help you. Pray that you're blessed with the presence of *moi.* I'm sorry. I'm not trying to be critical, but these are real people saying real words that sometimes make us smile because we are also real people.

* *The key that turns the lock is Romans 1:16-17. It's not short, but go ahead and handwrite the verses in the margin because it's important.*

At the end of the Book of Romans, Paul emphasizes the fact that he wants to come and visit them, and he asks for their prayer in getting him there. *ROSEEEE ...*

Then, he gets arrested in Jerusalem for his teaching, which makes for a long week.

SPREAD

Paul fights the charges by reminding them of all his credentials and after two years in prison he makes the case that he should go to Rome to be sentenced because he's Roman.

He really wants to go to Rome. Are you sensing that?

Basically the trial in Jerusalem got weird as soon as Paul appealed to Caesar in Rome. They didn't want to deal with all the fallout, so they agreed to send him on over to Rome where he would be granted rights as a Roman citizen.

Flip over to the Book of Acts to make sure all of this is still making sense in context. If your Bible has headings over sections, (and I hope it does. I tend to love that.), you'll see that chapter 27 is about Paul sailing for Rome. The next heading talks about a storm, and then a shipwreck. Paul is stranded in Malta for a while but eventually makes it to Rome. (YAY! Or … *yikes* …)

☐ EPHESIANS=
wisdom and practical advice for Christians living in the world

☐ PHILIPPIANS=
encouragement to rejoice, no matter the circumstances

While Paul hangs out in jail, he writes letters to the church in Ephesus, the church in Philippi, and the church in Colosse (You got it: Ephesians, Philippians, and Colossians). He also writes to an individual named Philemon.

I've got to hand it to Paul; he sure is an ambitious pen pal.

The Letter to the Ephesians was written to encourage them in their belief that Jesus offered them new life and power over sin.

* *What does Ephesians 3:1 tell us about the recipients of Paul's letter?*

He calls himself a "prisoner for Christ." Did you realize that he was actually a prisoner when he wrote to the Ephesians? Sure you did. I'm just checking. I love the Book of Ephesians. So much wisdom and practical application, even for today. You should read the whole thing. Keep in mind he is writing from a dark and difficult place, yet still urging them to walk "in a manner worthy of the calling to which you have been called," (4:1) and to be "imitators of God, as beloved children." (5:1)

But what about the Philippians? The Letter to the Philippians talks about how grateful Paul is for their support and encourages them to have joy as Christians regardless of their circumstances. When you read these words think about this: Paul is chained to a Roman soldier, and his letter to the church in Philippi is to remind them of the goodness of a faithful God.

 SPREAD

Those letters contain this message from a dark prison cell: Love Him. No matter what, love the Lord. In the final sentence in Ephesians, Paul says this: "Grace be with all who love our Lord Jesus Christ with love incorruptible" (Ephesians 6:24). Indeed.

His final letter to a church from this time in prison will be to the Colossians, and it's written around the same time as Ephesians and Philippians. The subject of Colossians, however, is a particular problem in the church. The believers at Colosse had been encouraging the worship of angels, and they put a heavy emphasis on Jewish ceremonies. Paul took this opportunity to remind them that Christ had freed them from the law, and that He was all in all.

In Colossians 2:16 Paul reminds them that they shouldn't allow people to pass judgment on them, and he lists several specific examples.

☐ COLOSSIANS = Christ freed us from the law

* *Given what you just learned about the purpose of this book, why do you think he mentioned these particular things?*

He wants them to remember that the divisions that used to exist were torn down in Christ.

* *Fill in the blanks from Colossians 3:11 "Here there is not _____ and _____, circumcised and _____, barbarian, Scythian, _____, _____; but Christ is all, and in all.*

Christ alone, Paul says.
And we should still be listening.

  SPREAD

DAY 3
PAUL'S LETTERS TO INDIVIDUALS

Paul has four more letters to write, but this time they are to specific individuals instead of churches. The first one, Philemon, is written during the same period as the few we just studied—while Paul is imprisoned in Rome.

Philemon is a teensy-tiny book—only 25 verses, to be exact. Find it in your Bible and read the first three verses. This shouldn't come out of left field at this point, but I want to make sure you're keeping up.

* *To whom is Paul writing the letter?*

Paul is an old man by now, according to his words in verse 9, an old man in his mid-to-late 50s. Life hadn't been kind to Paul. He is writing with a particular request for his friend Philemon. Philemon had a slave named Onesimus who had run away from him and providentially ended up in Rome where he met Paul. They became dear friends and brothers in Christ, and Paul is reaching out to Philemon and asking him to please accept Onesimus's return.

☐ PHILEMON=
a plea for a
brother in Christ

Slavery was common around the world during this time period, and Scripture reflects its place in history. Unfortunately, this means we have to look at one of the most horrifying acts of humankind—the belief that one can own and control another human being.

For the scope of this Bible study, it's not possible for me to spend as much time here as I'd like to. I don't want to be dismissive of the fact that this was (and still is) a very real tragedy that grieves the heart of God. What I do want to point out is the way Paul encourages Philemon to welcome Onesimus home.

* *Read Philemon 15-20.*

No longer a slave. A brother. Be reconciled with him, and let me take care of whatever he may owe you.

Here, nestled in the pit of a dark time, we see the light of Christ, our debt-taker, our ransom.

LETTERS

The year after he wrote to Philemon, Paul writes to his dear friend Timothy, the minister of an influential church in Ephesus. Paul is giving the young man advice on being a godly man and a devoted pastor. This book (along with the next two) is invaluable to pastors today as well as to anyone seeking to understand the way different church situations should be handled.

☐ 1 TIMOTHY= how to minister in the church

* *Paul's affection for Timothy is evident even from the opening lines of his letter, and he is quick to describe himself in accurate (although unflattering) ways in verses 1:12-17. What does he say about himself?*

Paul knows what he was, and he knows the only reason he isn't that anymore is because of the mercy of Jesus. But it wasn't just done for Paul's sake. He's careful to give the higher purpose behind his salvation.

* *What was Paul's purpose? (1 Timothy 1:16-17)*

Through Him and for Him. All of it. Shortly after writing his first letter to Timothy, Paul writes another pastor named Titus. Paul wrote these two letters during a time of freedom after he was imprisoned.

Titus was a Gentile bishop in Crete whom Paul had mentored. The church in Crete was experiencing a lot of struggle, so Paul had left Titus there to sort things out. Time passed and the apostle wrote to check on Titus and give him some advice to help him in his work. Specifically, Paul tells Titus how to choose good leaders, and lists qualifications that should be heeded.

☐ TITUS= advice on leadership

* *Read Titus 1:6-9 and list several attributes Paul mentions.*

The heart of Paul's message to Titus is this: those who say they are believers in Christ better have the actions to back it up.

Paul's final letter was a second message to his beloved son-in-the-faith Timothy, written from a last imprisonment in Rome. Many scholars believe Nero had Paul killed shortly after he wrote the letter, but Scripture is silent on it.

LETTERS

☐2 TIMOTHY=
the last letter of Paul

Of all Paul's letters, 2 Timothy pulls at my heart the most. I wouldn't have said that before I learned about the context, but now I can hardly read it without getting teary-eyed. The letter is the closest thing we have to a last will and testament from Paul, and although he likely knew he wouldn't survive much longer, I doubt he knew these would be his last words. In fact, at the end of the letter he urges Timothy to come and see him soon, although they probably never met in the flesh again.

Think about it: Paul had lived his life as a faithful servant, often imprisoned and tortured for his unwavering faith in the Christ he blatantly opposed early in his life. He traveled hundreds and hundreds of miles telling anyone who would listen, "I tell you this; I was blind but now I see."

With his body worn from time and weathered from hardship, he sits in the darkness of prison. The shadow of death covers him and he lifts his frail hand to write the words,

I am not ashamed, for I know whom
I have believed, and I am convinced
that he is able to guard until that Day
what has been entrusted to me.
2 TIMOTHY 1:12

Then, after several practical suggestions related to the church, Paul wrote a few sentences that have genuinely blessed me as much as any others in the Word. In my mind's eye, I see him crouched in the squalor of a pit and the beauty of his devotion stirs me.

He is speaking to Timothy, yes. But he is also, by the grace of God, speaking to you and me as disciples of Christ. Listen, will you?

* *Fill in your own name on the first line of verse 1 and verse 5. Use 2 Timothy 4:1-2, 5-7 to complete the rest.*

LETTERS

I charge you, _____, in the
presence of God and of Christ Jesus, who is to
judge the living and the dead, and by his appearing
and his kingdom: _____ the word; be
_____ in season and out of season;
reprove, rebuke, and _____,
with complete patience and teaching.
2 TIMOTHY 4:1-2

As for you, _____, always be
_____ _____,
endure _____, do
the work of an _____,
fulfill your _____.
2 TIMOTHY 4:5

Yes, Lord. May it be so.
     And may I say the same as Paul when I come to the end of my days
on this earth:

For I am already being poured out like a drink
offering, and the time of my departure has
come. I have fought the good fight, I have
finished the race, I have kept the faith.
2 TIMOTHY 4:6-7

Preach the word. Endure suffering. Fulfill the ministry God has given you.
     That's how you run your race; it's how you fight the good fight and
keep your faith.

* *What does reading this inspire in you? Spend your last*
  few minutes here today documenting in the margin
  anything the Lord has brought to mind.

 LETTERS

DAY 4
THE GENERAL LETTERS

People other than Paul wrote the next several Epistles. We call them the General Letters. The first one we're going to cover is the Book of James, written by the brother of Christ.

James may be the brother of Jesus (well, technically the half-brother), but he wasn't a follower of His while Christ was on the earth.

Yep, you read that right. He actually opposed Jesus and didn't become a believer until after the resurrection, when Jesus appeared to him and he converted.

☐ JAMES =
practical instruction on how to live as a Christian

So that's kind of the ultimate therapy session.

We are certain that James wrote the letter, but we aren't as sure about when he wrote it. Some scholars believe it was A.D. 47–48 which would make the Book of James possibly the earliest words of the New Testament written. Other Bible students argue that James wrote closer to A.D. 60–62. That's not really the end of the world, but I mention it just so you'll feel fancy at your small group.

✳ *To whom did James write? (James 1:1)*

James probably lived in Jerusalem. You might note that in Acts 15 he led what scholars call the Jerusalem conference where church leaders hammered out the fact that Gentiles didn't have to become Jews to become followers of Jesus. So James was, in effect, the senior pastor of the Jerusalem church.

James wrote to the Jewish Christians who lived outside of the holy land. And here's the thing with James: he's a practical guy. He gives solid instruction on how to live an obedient Christian life and warns of the perils that come from being lax in your faith.

James wrote five chapters packed with instruction. It reads like a New Testament version of Proverbs. The short book contains many often-quoted verses. I could spend the rest of the study on them, but instead I'll just pick a couple of doozies to give you the feel of it.

✳ *Read James 2:17. What does it say?*

LETTERS

A lot of confusion and debate in the church has surrounded that verse. Some people take it to mean that works lead to faith, while others say good works are evidence of solid faith. Because the New Testament is so clear about our salvation being through faith alone, I side with the latter.

In and of ourselves, no amount of good things we can do will save us. Even our most righteous acts are like filthy rags before a holy God (Isaiah 64:6). As Paul said to the Galatians, "A person is not justified by works of the law but through faith in Jesus Christ" (Galatians 2:16). We are made right by faith through the grace of God. Nothing more, nothing less.

Now there is something I should mention here, and that's this: if your life shows no "fruit" or "evidence" that you're a Christian, there's good reason to believe you're not actually a believer. Jesus tells us that you can tell a tree by its fruit—evidence that a person who says they believe in Christ will follow it up by acting like it.

* *James also warns us about the power of the tongue. According to James 3:8, who can tame his tongue?*

Oh good. That's encouraging.
    Don't worry. I'm going to wrap up James on a high note.

* *Write James 5:16, and embrace it as fact and truth. And then get to acting like you believe it is.*

OK, James. Thank you for all your wise words.

HEBREWS

Now we move to the Book of Hebrews, which was likely written around A.D. 63. But here's the catch: we don't know who wrote it.

People have theories. Some say Paul wrote Hebrews, and others say it might have been Barnabas or another friend of Timothy's. We don't have to know the author to appreciate the clear message. Hebrews encourages a group of Hebrew people (I bet you pieced that together without my help) to remain faithful to Christ in a time of persecution.

Hebrews proclaims the superiority of Jesus over, among other things, angels, the law, the temple, and the priesthood. Hebrews helps us appreciate a lot about Judaism and uses many Old Testament examples followed by the explanation of how they are fulfilled in Christ.

☐ HEBREWS=
    Jesus is the Prophet, Priest, and King

LETTERS

For example, read Hebrews 3:3. Who does the writer claim Jesus was greater than?

The writer goes on to present the case for believing that Jesus was in fact the ultimate High Priest and the ultimate Sacrifice that were "shadowed" in the Old Testament. They were pointing to Him, the Author and Perfecter of our faith.

The Book of Hebrews encourages us to have hope and to rest in our assurance of salvation. Chapter 11 contains what is often referred to as the "Hall of Faith," naming a series of people in Scripture who acted out of faith. Overall, the Book of Hebrews gives us a glimpse into the eternal Priesthood of Jesus Christ, who is seated at the right hand of the Father, the Ruler of a kingdom that cannot be shaken (Hebrews 8:1; 12:28-29).

1 & 2 PETER

Remember the disciple who denied Christ three times? Well, turns out he didn't just star in the first 12 chapters of Acts. Peter is back and writing two letters to Jewish Christians. The first one was written while he was being persecuted for his faith (around A.D. 63) and its goal is summarized in 1 Peter 1:3-5.

☐1 & 2 PETER=
perseverance in
the truth

What's the tone of these words? Write down any adjectives that come to mind.

In his second letter, he changes things up a bit. Read 2 Peter 3:1-7. Now how would you describe his tone?

A couple of years have passed and Peter wants to make sure they're warned. People will try to tear you from the truth, and you better be on guard.

Great work, Peter.

JUDE

The last book we're going to study today is Jude, and it's written by … OK, the drumroll may be unnecessary at this point.

LETTERS

Yep, Jude.

He's another half-brother of Christ who doesn't appear to have placed his faith in Jesus until His death either. His writing is very similar to Peter's and is obviously influenced by him. He also warns believers about the danger of false teachers. Go ahead and just skim the page (it's that short) of Jude's writing and you'll pick up on his intensity. At least he ends things with a nice little doxology. That kind of takes the edge off a little.

All right, I know this was a long day. I'm proud of you—really. And you've only got one more day of homework, so you're almost to the finish line.

Come on, finish strong.

It's what Paul would want.

☐ JUDE=
warnings about
false teachers

LETTERS

DAY 5
THE BOOKS OF JOHN

I'll be honest. I'm a little weepy about today. Mostly because the study is wrapping up but also because Revelation freaks me out just a wee bit.

What? Surely this is not the first time you've heard a Bible scholar say that, is it?

In unrelated news, I am not a Bible scholar.

But we've landed on the last author of the New Testament books, and you'll remember him from a Gospel we studied called John. Yes, ma'am. The disciple Jesus loved is going to wrap things up on the set today.

The first three books we're going to look at (briefly, because, well, they're brief) are 1, 2, and 3 John.

The first one is written around A.D. 90, and it's for all Christians. There are seven things we are encouraged to do as believers.

☐ 1 JOHN=
how to walk as Jesus walked

＊ *I'll give you the references and you write them down.*

1.　1 John 1:6-7

2.　1 John 1:8-9

3.　1 John 2:4

4.　1 John 2:6

5.　1 John 2:9-10

6.　1 John 2:15

7.　1 John 2:22

Let the record show that I tried to come up with a cute acronym but I failed. Ah well, grace prevails.

LETTERS

They're important, valuable tools for us to have as Christians, and John writes in such a unique and personal style that we can't help but appreciate his words. Even when he's warning Christians about antichrists, you still kind of want to have him over for coffee. He's not a pushover, don't get me wrong; he just has such a deep affection for Christ and the church that it spills into every crevice of his contributions in Scripture.

I also love that he uses the phrase, "little children," over and over in 1 John, because it makes me feel like he's a kind caretaker. Precious John, the beloved disciple of Jesus, offering his final words on behalf of his Master. It's just too good.

2 JOHN

Second John is written around the same time as 1 John, but it has a unique twist.

* *To whom is the letter addressed? (2 John 1:1-4)*

☐ 2 JOHN=
walk in truth and love

It's officially the only time a woman is the recipient of a letter in the New Testament, and credit goes to John. Even better, some (*yikes?*) of her children are following Christ. So that's good(ish).

It's a short letter and I can sum it up for you: walk in truth and love.

I can't take credit—that's the heading in my Bible. And also a great summary.

* *According to verses 5-6, what is the greatest commandment and how do we show it?*

3 JOHN

John's third letter is 15 verses long, so I think it's safe to say he was on his last leg. Not really, but kind of. I mean, John is old and he's nearing the end of his life. He picks up his pen to write to a dear friend and ministry partner named Gaius. I dare you to tell a pregnant person in your Bible study that you feel like the Lord is telling her to name the baby Gaius.

☐ 3 JOHN=
encouragement
to Gaius

No, don't, because these pranks can go wrong sometimes.

Gaius was a wonderful man of God, always generous and welcoming to people. He offered his possessions (including his home) to fellow

LETTERS

believers, and was the kind of guy you would want in your corner. Obviously he meant a lot to John, who pens this last letter in his honor to encourage him in his faith and tell him how much he wished he could see him.

This brings us to the last book of the Bible, and also the last book credited to John, although that statement bears a little clarification.

REVELATION

The Book of Revelation, written around the year A.D. 95, is the only book of prophesy in the New Testament. It was given to John by Christ Himself, who revealed what we as the church refer to as the "end times." Maybe you've seen the movie or read the books?

Or maybe you've studied the symbolism for years and have written dissertations on the bowls, the lamps, and the 144,000 of Israel who are sealed. If that is the case, I want to personally thank you for spending the past few weeks with me and encourage you to leave. Now.

Sorry, it's a coping mechanism. But I hope there's some part of you that is encouraged to know that a Bible scholar* like myself is a little intimidated by the Book of Revelation.

When John wrote the Book of Revelation, he was an elderly man and the only one of the 12 disciples who was still alive. He had been banished to an island called Patmos as a punishment for preaching the gospel. His beloved fellow believers were suffering persecution under the Roman government.

In a series of visions, Jesus shows John several things. He gives glimpses of what will happen in the future. He challenges the suffering believers to remain faithful. And he clearly portrays the judgment that is to come on the Devil and his minions. Jesus Christ will defeat Satan forever. Like, he's done. The triumphant Lord will return to earth as He predicted, taking His place on the throne as the King for all time. A new heaven and a new earth will descend, and within this kingdom will be the New Jerusalem. There won't be any sadness, any sin, or any death; and believers will spend eternity with our Savior.

Deep in our bones we long for this place, even if we cannot comprehend it from our present circumstances.

As spectacular as the garden of Eden was, it will pale in comparison to what God has planned for us. The fallen, crooked world will be made right, and none of the brokenness will remain.

And so we wait.

Only four words, but they say it all.

Not actually a Bible scholar.

□ REVELATION =
prophecy about the
end of the world and
the new earth

REVELATION

We've heard about Him from the first sentence, and we've loved Him without seeing Him. We've questioned, prayed, imagined, believed, hoped for, and learned, and yet, it's all been a shadow compared to what is to come.

There's a weariness that accompanies our steps here—an inexplicable homesickness that reminds us that, quite simply, we aren't home yet.

All the words of the Bible are a love song to us, the beloved bride of Christ.

We don't know when, and we can't fathom how, but we rest our hope on the unshakable kingdom that is yet to be.

How do we end a study that has brought us all the way through Scripture? What's next?

I'm so glad you asked.

God's last words to John are carved in my heart, their power coming to life through the pages of His seamless story:

"Surely I am coming soon."

All of these words, all of the promises and adventures, they have served their purpose: to point us to our great God. And with that, we look onward and upward, eagerly awaiting His glorious return.

And until then, beloved …

Make your life an offering to the King.

I can't think of a better way to end our time together than to simply repeat John's response to Christ, praying that it will become etched on your heart as the bright hope of your life on earth.

Amen. Come, Lord Jesus!

The grace of the Lord Jesus be with you all.

Amen.

REVELATION

SESSION 7 THE LETTERS

REVIEW WEEK 6 HOMEWORK

* Day 1: What promise that Paul extended to the young believers at Thessalonica (see 1 Thessalonians 4:13-18) means the most to you?

  • What that Paul said about himself in 2 Corinthians 11:22-33 impressed you?

  • Based on Galatians 2:16, what justifies a person?

* Day 2: What does Colossians 3:11 mean to you?

* Day 3: What sort of lives (actions) should believers have to back up their belief?

  • Why should we be willing to endure suffering in order to fulfill the ministry God has given us?

* Day 4: Why is taming the tongue such an important issue for believers?

  • Why is James 5:16 so important for us as believers?

* Day 5: What did you discover about the apostle John this week?

  • According to verses 2 John 5-6, what is the greatest commandment and how do we show it?

#seamlessbiblestudy

WATCH SESSION 7: THE LETTERS (VIDEO RUN TIME: 11:21)

DISCUSS

* How does Paul's story bring you hope? Inspire you? Challenge you?

* Are you trusting God to use your life for His purposes in this world? Explain.

* How can difficult times bring us closer to Christ? When have you seen that happen in your own life?

* Do you believe God is everything He says He is? Do you trust Him? If so, how are you living your life to tell His story?

Video sessions available for purchase at *www.lifeway.com/seamless*

CONTINUE IN BIBLE STUDY

Perhaps you are new to Bible study and have questions about the best way to learn more. Hopefully, you have fallen in love with Scripture during this study and want to dive in deeper.

Similar Bible studies keep you connected to believers who are learning from God's Word, too. They provide you a specific time and place to focus on some aspect of the Bible and its application to life. However, nothing compares to a daily personal encounter with God. Here are some reasons and benefits. We study the Bible to:

- Know the truth. We want to think clearly about what God says is true and valuable (see 2 Pet. 1:20-21).

- Know God in a personal relationship (see 1 Cor. 1:21; Gal. 4:8-9; 1 Tim. 4:16).

- Live well for God in this world. Living out His will expresses our love for Him (see John 14:23-24; Rom. 12:2; 1 Thess. 4:1-8; 2 Tim. 3:16-17).

- Experience God's freedom, grace, peace, hope, and joy (see Ps. 119:111; John 8:32; Rom. 15:4; 2 Pet. 1:2).

- Grow spiritually as we reject conformity to the world and are changed by the renewing of our minds (see Rom. 12:2; 1 Pet. 2:1-2).

- Minister to other Christ followers and to those who have yet to respond to the gospel (see Josh. 1:8; 2 Tim. 2:15; 3:16-17; Eph. 6:11-17; 2 Pet. 2:1-2).

- Guard ourselves from sin and error (see Eph. 6:11-17; 2 Pet. 2:1-2).

- Build up as a Christian community with others in the body of Christ (see Acts 20:32; Eph. 4:14-16).[1]

If you do not already have a daily quiet time, commit to selecting a special time and place. Choose the time of day that works best for you, and make it a priority. Keep your Bible and study materials in your meeting place. Develop a balanced plan for Bible reading, such as A Reader's Guide to the Bible.[2] Make notes to see how God is speaking, and respond to Him in prayer. Strive for consistency as your main goal.[3]

1. George H. Guthrie, *Read the Bible for Life* (Nashville: LifeWay Press, 2010), 16.
2. "A Reader's Guide to the Bible" can be found in *Read the Bible for Life* by George H. Guthrie.
3. George H. Guthrie, *Read the Bible for Life* (Nashville: LifeWay Press, 2010), 18.

START A TOOLBOX

As you can, begin to build a Bible study toolbox of resources to enhance your understanding of the Bible. A good study Bible in an understandable translation is essential. In choosing a Bible translation, look for one that uses the earliest and most reliable Hebrew and Greek manuscripts. Some translations seek to approximate word-for-word correspondence with the Hebrew or Greek text while others seek to capture the sense of the author's intended meaning in highly readable language.[3] Other helpful tools are a concordance and Bible dictionary.

Here are features of each Bible study tool to enhance your study:

BIBLE ATLAS—Maps, charts, and photographs that illustrate the land, sites, and archaeology of the ancient world of the Bible

BIBLE DICTIONARY—Alphabetical list of key terms, places, people, events, and concepts in the Bible

BIBLE ENCYCLOPEDIA—Articles about Bible characters, events, and places, including history, religious environment, culture, language, and literature, as well as cross-references to related Scripture verses

BIBLE HANDBOOK—Brief commentary, maps, historical background, archaeological background, kings, genealogies, and other information about the Bible.

BIBLE COMMENTARY—Detailed theological analysis of specific verses and passages of Scripture. Includes a background introductory section for each book of the Bible, followed by detailed commentary of Scripture verse by verse

BIBLE CONCORDANCE—Alphabetical index of important words in Scripture and the references of texts in which they are found

TOPICAL BIBLE—Bible references to topics addressed or mentioned in the Bible

ONLINE RESOURCES—The website *www.mystudybible.com* offers free online tools for reading and studying the Bible.[4]

---

4. Ibid., 23.
5. Adapted from *Read the Bible for Life Leader Kit*. Item 005253507. Published by LifeWay Press®. © 2010 George H. Guthrie. Made in the USA. Reproduction rights granted.

BEGIN TO MEMORIZE SCRIPTURE

As you develop in your understanding of the meaning of Scripture, consider committing verses to memory. You will be surprised how often a word from God comes to mind at just the right time. Here are some steps to get started:

BEGIN WITH A POSITIVE ATTITUDE.—Many people think they cannot memorize, but you can do all things through Christ (Phil. 4:13).

GLUE THE REFERENCE TO THE FIRST WORDS.—To remember both the verse and the references, say the reference and the first words without pausing. For example, "Philippians 4:13—I can do all things."

MEMORIZE BITE BY BITE.—Memorizing a verse phrase by phrase is easy because you are only learning five or six words at a time.

REVIEW, REVIEW, REVIEW.—Consider using memory cards to review. After memorizing the verse, review every day for 90 days, weekly for the next six weeks, and monthly for the rest of your life.

MEDITATE ON THE VERSE.—Meditation can increase your grasp of the passage's teaching and application.

USE SPARE TIME WISELY.—Use your mobile devices or carry Scripture-memory cards to use during your spare time or when exercising or waiting in line.

TEAM WITH A FRIEND.—Listen to each other's verse, checking the Bible or card for accuracy.[1]

Adapted from Read the Bible for Life Leader Kit. *Item 005253507. Published by LifeWay Press®.*
© 2010 George H. Guthrie. Made in the USA. Reproduction rights granted.

1. Thomas D. Lea, *God's Transforming Word: How to Study Your Bible* (Nashville: LifeWay Press, 1986), 12-13. Out of print.

Stop by Our Online Home

We have resources to help you grow in your faith, develop as a leader, and encourage you as you go. Visit us online to find Bible studies, podcasts, events, and more!

lifeway.com/women

LifeWay | Women

Books from

Chasing God

Maybe you've never asked the question out loud, but you've wondered. You do the things that look good on paper. But you aren't convinced you really know Him. Angie Smith understands, because she had run circles around the same paths searching for Him, frustrated at her lack of progress. She realized she wasn't following God, but instead trying to catch up with him. And without realizing it, you may be as well. | *978-1-4336-7661-1*

I Will Carry You

Advised to terminate the pregnancy of their fourth daughter, Angie Smith and her husband Todd chose instead to carry this child and allow room for a miracle. That miracle came the day they met Audrey Caroline and got the chance to love her for the precious two-and-a-half hours she lived on earth. | *978-0-8054-6428-3*

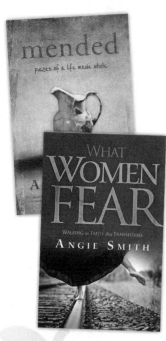

Mended

We love to cheer for the underdog and believe to our core that every life makes a difference. Yet, when it comes to the places of our innermost sense of shame and regret, we often wonder if it is really true that God can work all things together for good for those who love Him. | *978-1-4336-7660-4*

What Women Fear

A woman's faith in God is challenged by the first question Satan asks Eve in the Bible. That seed of doubt and the story it begins to unfold breed a concept of fear still haunting each of us on some level every day-the idea that our actions could ruin something beautiful, and God might not have control of things. | *978-0-8054-6429-0*

Every WORD Matters®
BHPublishingGroup.com

ANGIE SMITH

For Such a Time As This

Angie Smith and Breezy Brookshire have teamed up on *For Such a Time as This*, a Bible storybook for girls that features 40 biblical retellings from prominent women in both the Old and New Testament. Girls aged 6 to 10 will enjoy learning about God through the recounts of the Bible's heroines and stunning illustrations. Summaries at the end of each story highlight the attribute of God to be learned and offer thoughtful reflections for both parent and child to takeaway. | 978-1-4336-8046-5

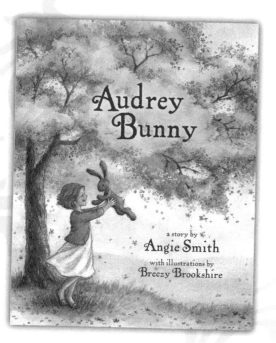

Audrey Bunny

In this sweet children's book, a stuffed animal, named Audrey Bunny, fears her imperfections make her unworthy of a little girl's love. She'll learn the truth soon enough, and young readers will learn that everyone is special and wonderfully made by God.
978-1-4336-8045-8

B&H KIDS

EVERY *little* WORD MATTERS®
BHKidsBuzz.com